GHOST TOWN
STORIES OF BC

GHOST TOWN STORIES OF BC

Tales of Hope, Heroism and Tragedy

JOHNNIE BACHUSKY

VICTORIA · VANCOUVER · CALGARY

Heritage House Publishing Company Ltd.
www.heritagehouse.ca

Library and Archives Canada Cataloguing in Publication
Bachusky, Johnnie
    Ghost town stories of BC: tales of hope, heroism and tragedy / Johnnie Bachusky. — 1st Heritage House ed.

1st ed. published Canmore, Alta.: Altitude Pub. Canada, 2004 under title Ghost town stories III.
Includes bibliographical references.
ISBN 978-1-894974-73-8

    1. Ghost towns — British Columbia — History. 2. British Columbia — History, Local. I. Title.

FC3820.G4 B32 2009   971.1   C2009-900134-9

Series editor: Lesley Reynolds.
Cover design: Chyla Cardinal. Interior design: Frances Hunter.
Cover photo: Sandon, Johnnie Bachusky. Interior photos: all photographs by the author, except page 56, courtesy of Nobuyoshi Hayashi; page 70, courtesy of the Adolph Sercu family living in Belgium; page 116, courtesy of the Gordon Carlson family; and page 128, courtesy of Joe Van Raalte.

 Mixed Sources
Cert no. SW-COC-001271
© 1996 FSC
FSC

The interior of this book was produced using 100% post-consumer recycled paper, processed chlorine free and printed with vegetable-based inks.

Heritage House acknowledges the financial support for its publishing program from the Government of Canada through the Canada Book Fund (CBF), Canada Council for the Arts and the province of British Columbia through the British Columbia Arts Council and the Book Publishing Tax Credit.

 Canada Council Conseil des Arts
for the Arts du Canada

 BRITISH COLUMBIA
ARTS COUNCIL
Supported by the Province of British Columbia

12 11 10   2 3 4 5

For my brother Wayne

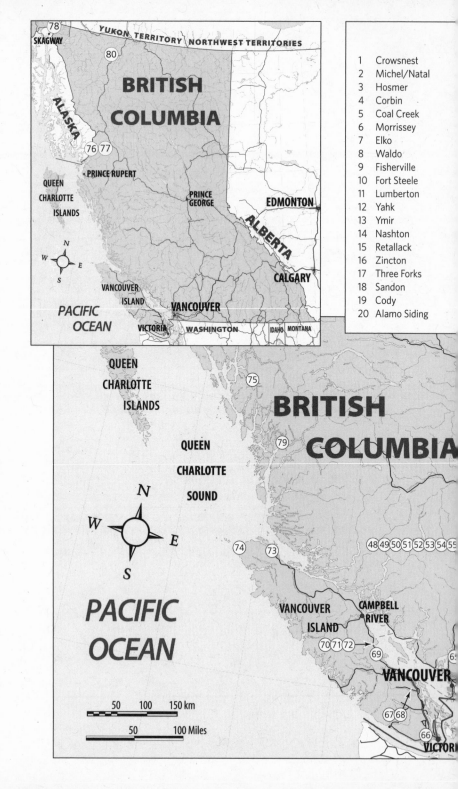

Ghost Towns of British Columbia

Historic St. Saviour's Anglican Church in Barkerville

Contents

Prologue

Martin Haller sat at the side of the dusty road, cradling a .32 Winchester Special. He lifted his head from his gnarled hands and looked towards Waldo's Krag Hotel. With a determined look, he lurched to his feet and hoisted the rifle. Muttering to himself, he set off towards the hotel. He was broke and desperate. He had lost everything at the poker table, and he hadn't had a job for months—ever since Billy Palmer had fired him from the Krag. Revenge raged in his ice-cold veins. Someone was going to pay for his misery, he vowed.

Reaching the hotel porch, he pumped his rifle then pushed through the Krag's front door, swung right and went striding into the saloon. Billy Palmer was tending bar. Martin glared at Billy and shouted, "I'm here looking for you!" The laughter and conversation in the room stopped dead. Billy stared right back at Martin, then glanced quickly into his office, just three metres away, where his own rifle was leaning against the wall. As Billy made a dash for his weapon, Martin aimed at his enemy and fired.

Distant Voices

ONE SUNNY WEEKEND DURING THE summer of 1988, Fernie historian John Kinnear and photographer Lawrence Chrismas hiked along an old road leading to the ghost town of Coal Creek, eight kilometres east of Fernie, BC. Lawrence, a photographer who is known nationally for his striking portraits of coal miners, paused to reflect on the beauty of the wilderness surrounding them. As his gaze came back to the road, he noticed something small poking out of the ground. He pried it from its resting place and discovered it was a rare 1898 coin.

The two men were excited about their 90-year-old find. They chatted about it and assumed it had belonged to an early Coal Creek resident. For John, a mining technician for a local coal company, it was a defining moment. He felt that finding the coin, a symbol of the past, was a message that the past should be saved from obliteration. He began to realize that the mining heritage of British Columbia would be lost unless he and others did something to save it. He knew there were other mining ghost towns in British Columbia's Crowsnest Pass that had either already been erased or were in danger of being lost because too few cared about preserving them.

Since that day, John and Lawrence have been two of the few who cared. They began working together on the history and heritage committee of the Coal Association of Canada. They also toured coal mines throughout the Crowsnest Pass, Nordegg and central east Alberta, then promoted and documented each one.

John has been drawn back to Coal Creek many times. He has searched through the few remaining ruins hoping to find some meaningful reminders that this was once a vibrant community. With each visit, John is saddened. He has found only scattered mounds of concrete and bits of rusty steel.

The historian has gained some sense of the past by studying the mine's record books. He is astonished at the cross-section of nationalities that came to Coal Creek at the turn of the 20th century. Sadly, many of these immigrants lost their lives working in the deplorably dangerous mines.

Unfortunately, most former residents of Coal Creek and other pioneer communities across British Columbia have

All that is left of Coal Creek are bits and pieces of old machinery, pipes, metal and concrete. The coal-mining ghost town, eight kilometres east of Fernie, was closed forever in 1958.

passed on, so they can't tell us their stories first-hand. But the stories we have, whether tragic, whimsical, inspirational or bizarre, are all intriguing. They deserve to be told.

Every few years I take a trip to the Valley of the Ghosts in the West Kootenays. From the former townsite of Nashton, a few kilometres west of Kaslo, to the forlorn pair of roadside mine buildings at Retallack, the haunting structural relics at Cody and on to the spectacular collapsed mine-site ruins of Alamo Siding, I sense John's sadness. Each time I pass these pioneer settlements, the old buildings are a little more weather-beaten and forlorn. Somewhere in the haunting wind that rattles through each relic, there are voices still waiting to be heard.

I get the same feeling in the Boundary Country, the Lardeau district, the Gold Rush Trail, Bridge River Valley, the Lower Mainland and on Vancouver Island—all filled with undocumented voices of British Columbia's past.

More than 15 years after they found that old coin, John and Lawrence continue with their quest to make sure these distant voices are heard. And now, so do I.

Heroes

BILL MILBURN'S EYES WELLED WITH tears as he accepted the coveted trophy. The hardy coal miner had reached his personal goal. He, along with his six teammates and coach, Jazz Anderson, had just won the first Dominion Mine Rescue Championship.

The trophy cup had an old miner's safety lamp welded onto it. This lamp, an original, was one of the first used in the Coal Creek mines, where Bill, his father and his grandfather had toiled for so many years. To Bill, it was a cherished symbol of his life's work.

"I was determined I was going to win a trophy with the lamp on it because it was used at Coal Creek all those years," says Bill, still touched by the memory of the 1967 win. "With it being the first Canadian championship that we were ever going to have, I didn't care if I won any more, as long as I won that one."

He is justifiably proud of that achievement. The Michel, BC, men defeated five crack teams from across Canada that day. But there was another deeply personal reason for Bill's joy. A month earlier, his 27-year-old brother, Walter, had been killed, along with 15 other miners, during an explosion at the Balmer North Mine in Michel. Bill's championship win was for Walter.

Bill, who is now enjoying a well-earned retirement in Fernie, grew up in Coal Creek and began working in the mines as a lad of 17. For 12 years, until the mine closed in 1958, he worked in the company barn taking care of the mine horses, shoeing them and driving them into the mine. Without the mine for employment, Bill and the other miners had to leave. It wasn't long before Coal Creek became a ghost town. Within a few years, most of the buildings would be torn down or moved, and the wilderness would slowly begin reclaiming the site.

Bill moved to Michel in the Crowsnest Pass, about 50 kilometres east of Coal Creek. He began working in the mine there and was soon asked to join the rescue team. Saving lives became Bill's cherished duty. After proving himself in a series of rescues, he was asked to captain the team. As well as performing daring rescues on the job, the men entered rescue competitions. Bill led them to a pair of second-place provincial honours and one third-place finish before taking them on to the 1967 championship.

Rescue missions were in Bill's blood and a major part of Coal Creek's glorious but sometimes heartbreaking past. His grandfather, Joe, who first moved to Coal Creek from England in 1903, had been a first-aid runner during the First World War until he was badly wounded by enemy shrapnel. Despite his injuries, he returned to Canada to dig coal at Coal Creek.

Joe had known he could be in as much danger underground as he had been on the battlefield. He had witnessed accidents in the mine and heard about the terrible disaster of 1902. It had struck at 7:30 p.m. on May 29.

On that spring evening, an explosion rocked the No. 2 mine at the Coal Creek Colliery. The force of the blast extended to No. 3 mine. It was so powerful that the air and coal dust, along with rocks and chunks of coal, were forced back through the fan house, carrying away the foot of the building. A column of dust and rocks catapulted more than 300 metres into the air, fanning out before dropping debris across one side of the mountain. There were more than 150 miners on that evening shift.

The mine's rescue teams tried to get to their stricken colleagues hundreds of metres below, but were overcome by noxious gases known as "afterdamp." Despite the dangers, rescue crews worked in four-hour shifts to repair the air ducts so the deadly gases could be cleared.

All night and into the next morning, volunteers worked feverishly to remove the gas and allow rescuers into the poisoned mine. Men collapsed every few minutes and had to be replaced by fresh volunteers. Their heroic efforts were to no avail. Less than four hours after the initial blast, the first miner, a 13-year-old boy named Wil Robertson, was found. To the rescuers' despair, the boy was dead. Wil and another 129 miners had died instantly when they'd inhaled the poisonous gas. Only 20 miners escaped.

A subsequent inquest heard the explosion was likely caused by the build-up of dangerous gas at the coalface. The inquest's jury was also told the explosion was "extended and intensified" by dust that had collected to dangerous levels because of inadequate procedures for removing and watering dust in the mine.

To this day, the Coal Creek mine explosion is still one of the worst mine disasters in Canadian history. Although it was the worst, it certainly wasn't the last. In 1917, another explosion in No. 3 mine killed 34 men. Eleven years later, a blowout claimed another six lives.

At intervals in Coal Creek's six-decade history, scores of miners were injured and several killed by a phenomenon called "the bump." This infamous phenomenon, which always started in mine No. 1 east, was caused by trapped pressurized underground gases.

Bill still has a clear picture in his mind of what the bump did to the underground tunnels. "The floor came up and hit the roof. It would flatten the coal mine cars out to nothing," he explains. "It was like an earthquake. It used to shake all of the houses. You could hear the cups rattling and everything. You could feel it all the way to Fernie."

Another former resident of Coal Creek, Grace Arbuckle, remembers the terror the miners' families felt whenever the dreaded bump reverberated through the town. She says they raced from their homes to the bottom of the hill, just under the entrance of No. 1 east mine, and comforted each other while black coal dust poured out of the mine's fan. They watched anxiously as management officials assessed the damage and potential injuries, or worse still, fatalities.

Grace, who had four brothers working in the mines, remembers one of those bumps particularly well, even though it happened 60 years ago. Her brother Johnny was working in the No. 1 east mine when the bump caused an explosion and cave-in. Johnny was trapped.

"My dad hadn't been in the mine for years," Grace says, "but he went in to find Johnny. They told him not to build his hopes up, but after searching down below he said he heard him groan. He knew as soon as they hit a certain part in that mine that Johnny was alive. Mine rescue dug him out, but my dad was there."

Grace was grateful her brother was spared, but felt deeply for other families who were not as lucky. "I don't know if you can imagine what it feels like to know your own is coming out and your neighbour's isn't," she says.

But Grace has happier memories of her former home and describes it fondly. She lived in the bustling creekside community with her parents and nine siblings from 1920 to 1939. It was laid out in subdivisions, one for each ethnic group, such as Welsh Camp and French Camp, where she and her family lived in a three-bedroom private home.

The mountain community grew rapidly, with its mine and townsite stretching at least a kilometre along the banks of Coal Creek. With an estimated population of about 1,000 people by 1905, the townsite quickly developed most of the amenities a small town needs, including churches, a three-room school, a store, boarding houses and "the club." The official name of the club was the Coal Creek Literary and Athletic Association; it was the social centre of the community. It had a bar for the thirsty miners, which was open even on Sundays, an unheard-of practice in the first half of the 20th century. There was also a library, a gymnasium and a dance hall with a kitchen.

There was also a sports field, a well-used facility where Coal Creekers played soccer and held picnics during the summers. In the winters, the men flooded part of the field and made an outdoor skating rink—much to the delight of the children. Some years before the mine closed, a free passenger-train service to Fernie was made available. The Golden Goose, as the train was called, offered a welcome break from the isolation.

Grace says Coal Creek residents lived harmoniously.

In fact, there was never a need to have a police detachment there. Every once in a while an incident rattled the community and citizens called in the law from Fernie. These incidents were a source of gossip and storytelling, especially for the kids. Grace recalls two of her favourites.

"When we were kids we heard that Tony Over-The-Top, an old bachelor, was robbed by a young man who stole his groceries. Tony took a shotgun and fired it so that it would only hurt the robber's foot. He shot him—and he never lost any more groceries. The young man limped around for awhile but he didn't lose his foot."

Grace and many other Coal Creek children especially enjoyed the story of the Benson ghost. (This 1912 tale was so sensational it was reported in the local newspapers.) Benson was an Englishman who came to work at the mine as a digger. He didn't get along with his boss, Mr. Joyce. To make matters worse, Joyce demoted the Englishman. Benson was furious and went to the club to get drunk. Before long, he was telling everyone in the bar that he was going to kill Joyce. The other patrons, not surprisingly, didn't take him seriously. But serious he was. Benson left the bar, got his revolver and went to Joyce's office.

"Now that I've got you on an even keel, I've got you where I want you," he shouted at the alarmed fire boss. The drunken man shot at Joyce, then panicked and ran. A search party set out to look for him. They found him lying by the railway tracks, dead. He had shot himself.

Meanwhile, Joyce was very much alive; Benson's bullet had only wounded him. Ironically, while Benson was drowning his sorrows, the mine superintendent had told Joyce to give the Englishman a better job. Since that time, many Coal Creekers have sworn Benson's ghost haunts that section of the railway tracks.

"One girl said she was out walking with her boyfriend and she felt somebody pulling her towards the mountain backwards," says Grace. "And old Mr. Carmichael once said he saw the ghost of Mr. Benson and ran home, breaking all the speed records. That was the biggest laugh of the town with the kids because he had to have a change of underwear when he got home."

Bill Milburn knows the ghost story, too. But it didn't affect him as much as a dramatic experience he had in 1951, when he was still working with the mine horses. The incident marked the beginning of his fame as a rescue worker.

On September 21—the first day of autumn and a day off for Bill—he was woken at 6:30 a.m. by a knock at the door. Several men crowded into the room and asked him to supply some horses and join them on a rescue mission into the wilderness, 15 kilometres east of Coal Creek. A group of Americans had been hunting in the mountains when one member of their party got badly hurt in an accident. His friends had carried him back to their camp, but could not get him down the mountain without horses and experienced help. Unless the rescue party reached him soon, it was feared the man would die.

It had snowed the night before and the going was tough for men and horses. The horses' hooves became clogged with ice and snow, causing them to slip on the steep incline. "We had to go eight miles into muskeg, along a side hill and no road; just an old pack trail," says Bill. "It was tiring and we hadn't had a chance to eat before we left."

The rescue team, which included a doctor, eventually reached the injured man. They were about to tend to the hunter when fate dealt them a nasty blow. One of the horses standing nearby slipped and rolled on top of the already injured man, crushing his abdomen. Both the Americans and the Coal Creek men were devastated. "The doctor put him out with a couple of shots and told us that he wasn't going to pull through," says Bill, with a shake of his head.

The rescue team began the ordeal of packing the man out to Coal Creek, taking turns carrying the stretcher. Fortunately for everyone, the horse was gentle, walking steadily along the trails. The rescue team switched men every five to ten minutes to conserve their energy. Thankfully, the injured man was unconscious throughout. His partners accompanied the rescuers, but they were still in shock, so were not much help.

"We were packing through scrubs and everything, getting cramps in the tops of our legs and trying to keep the stretcher level," says Bill. "We could only go 50 feet and someone would have to spell you off."

After six gruelling hours, they got back to Coal Creek.

From there, the man was taken to the hospital in Fernie. Sadly, he died two days later. "I still feel bad that he passed away, but we couldn't have got him down any quicker," says Bill. However, it's evident that their efforts were appreciated. Later, the man's wife came to the Coal Creek club to thank them.

This was not the first time Bill had experienced the bitter sorrow of not being able to save someone. Even before he joined the rescue team he had taken part in rescues in the Coal Creek mine. It was part of the miners' code that everyone took part in rescue operations in emergencies. As the years went by, he had more heartbreaking experiences. There were the rescue attempts where he and his teammates brought out bodies, not living men, and there were the terrible personal losses.

Bill and his cousin, Jazz Anderson, who was also Bill's rescue-team coach, were typical of families who lost many friends and close relatives to the dangerous work of mining. In the 1920s, Pete Anderson, Jazz's father, was killed by a falling rock in a mine at Mountain Park, Alberta; in the 1930s, John Milburn, uncle to both Jazz and Bill, was killed during a bump at Coal Creek; in the 1940s, another bump at Coal Creek claimed the life of George Anderson, Jazz's brother. A few years later, John Cairns, Jazz's brother-in-law, was killed during a cave-in at No. 1 east mine. The terrible list ended with the death of Bill's brother Walter at the Michel mine in 1967.

Although the losses weighed heavily on both men, they continued to dedicate their lives to saving others, no matter what the cost to themselves, and to celebrate their many triumphs. One of the last rescues the cousins worked on together was a widely reported mine disaster. This victory was won over great odds.

On June 19, a flood in the Balmer South Mine claimed three lives and left another three miners trapped. The men who survived the initial flood—fire boss John Krall, second operator Donald Evans and mechanic Frank Kutcher—were trapped in a four-metre by four-metre tunnel enclave. With typical bravado, the trio would later call this cold, dark deathtrap "Our Hotel Windsor."

When the flood hit, Donald had been quite a distance from John and Frank. He had been working with another man, Robert Dancoisne. Clinging to a shuttle car, Donald watched in horror as his friend was swept away by the surging torrent. The force of the water soon pulled Donald loose and swept him away as well. He was being carried along the mine's main supply road, towards the other two men. With only a third-of-a-metre airspace between the tunnel roof and the exploding water, he made his way towards the other survivors by pulling himself along roof air pipes.

At one point during this perilous journey through the pitch dark, he slammed into a large pile of jammed timbers. Though stunned by the blow, he managed to hang on to the pipes and eventually find his way to John and Frank.

Amazingly, he still had the strength to climb into the enclave where they were crouching.

While this drama was unfolding underground, Jazz Anderson, who was now the superintendent of Michel mines, was organizing the rescue. He summoned Bill to help. They soon discovered that all routes to the trapped miners were blocked. On that first day of the rescue mission, Jazz instructed his helpers to drill a hole to where he thought the missing miners might be. He then told Bill to insert a pipe down the hole and blow garlic powder through it. He hoped the smell would give the trapped men a signal that help was on the way. Unfortunately, the flow of garlic powder missed its mark and went in the opposite direction from where the stricken men were trapped.

Jazz then called for a "monkey crosscut" to be driven through the point where he was certain the miners were trapped. It took 48 hours of dangerous blasting and hand mining to reach the trio. By then, the men had been trapped for more than 84 horrific hours.

"As soon as we broke through, Jazz wanted the ladder and he went down," says Bill. Fortunately, Jazz's instinct proved right. Miraculously, the men were still alive. Bill finishes the story with a flourish. "He brought them up!"

The year after that incredible victory, Bill injured his back. His rescue work was over. He continued working at the Michel mine, first as a carpenter and then as the warehouse foreman, until he retired in 1984.

But that was not the end of his association with mining. He is still contributing to the mining community by keeping its history alive. He regales locals and coal-mining history enthusiasts alike with his first-hand reports of rescues and of Coal Creek's glory days. His listeners see Bill as a hero. Bill sees himself simply as a man who did what he could to help his fellow miners.

The Legendary Finks

CHARLIE FINK IS NOT A typical mayor from a typical town. In truth, Charlie and his town—Hosmer, BC—are as atypical as it gets. The short, slight, elderly legend lives in Hosmer's oldest house, a nearly century-old relic in the lowest part of town. Charlie has been impeached, vilified over worm digging and (while perched on a beer keg) publicly humiliated by his peers. And this is all good. Locals would be aghast if any of their mayors exhibited signs of dignity, fame, fortune or political skill.

Charlie has been the most popular mayor in the history of Hosmer, a place that in large part was a ghost town for most of the 20th century. He is also the last surviving Fink from Hosmer's pioneer days. Charlie's family first came to

Hosmer at a time when predictions abounded about Hosmer becoming the coal-mining jewel of BC's Crowsnest Pass. But the glory days were short-lived, and Hosmer was soon seized by ghosts. The Finks, nevertheless, went on to become local legends.

Residents elected Charlie as mayor several times, even after trying to impeach him in 1983. That year, Charlie thought it would be a good idea to turn the first sod for a new Hosmer fire hall. He was mayor, after all. But he'd forgotten one important detail: Hosmer politicians are not allowed to do any good deeds. In fact, they are not allowed to do anything—no exceptions, not even for their beloved Charlie. That's the Hosmer rule.

Caught in the act with shovel in hand, Charlie protested vociferously with his accusers that he was only digging for fishing worms. He even pulled out his fishing licence. It was not good enough to keep Charlie from being charged with digging for worms without a Hosmer Protection of Wildlife permit. Townsfolk dragged him to the local Elk River Hotel to hold a public trial. For Charlie's big day in court, town sheriff Terry Steabner dressed the beleaguered mayor in a long white smock and added a little halo above his head. The now-angelic Charlie was put on the prisoner's box, which looked awfully like a beer keg. Indignant jurors denounced him even before the proceedings began. Fortunately, Charlie got a big break when his lawyer, Neil Thompson, clamorously objected to the Crown's leading evidence—a pile of dried-up worms.

"These can't be the real worms!" boomed Neil. "If they were, they'd still be wiggling!" Then, in front of the startled jury and public gallery, he dipped the dehydrated creatures in beer and downed them.

"And you can't hang an angel!" he shrieked to the hoots and laughter from the fired-up Hosmer citizenry. With the evidence gone, the case zoomed to a close. Charlie was found not guilty. He resumed his term, promising never again to do any anything that blighted the quirky image of Hosmer.

In the years following 1983, the town gave Charlie a break from mayordom now and again by electing a dog, a four-year-old boy and even a visiting fly fisherman from the United States, whose real-life job as a prison warden was considered a highly desirable qualification for mayor.

"I like to think of us as one big, somewhat dysfunctional family," explains Hosmer resident Glenn Wallman, a former mayoralty campaign manager for Casey the Goat.

Certifiably dysfunctional or not, Hosmer is certainly one unique community, a motley collection of about 380 resource industry folks, entrepreneurs, artists, historians and schoolteachers who live in eccentric bliss halfway between Fernie and Sparwood in BC's Elk Valley. Hosmerites don't even acknowledge that Fernie and Sparwood are the predominant communities in their corner of the province. Rather, Fernie (10 kilometres south) is known as Hosmer South; Sparwood (10 kilometres north) is Hosmer North.

Hosmer's rise to brief fame began in 1906 when the settlement was established by the Canadian Pacific Railway. The town was a vital link in a long line of coal-mining communities that sprang up along the Alberta side of the Crowsnest Pass and westward into BC's Elk Valley.

By 1908, a comprehensive coal-mining site at Hosmer, intended to supply coke to the CPR's smelter at Trail, BC, was under construction. It included a tipple, boiler house, machine shops, powerhouse and magnificent array of 240 coke ovens.

With the promise of prosperity imminent, the building of a townsite was well underway by 1910. The new community soon reached a population of almost 1,300, with two residential sections, four hotels, a hospital, several churches and an opera house that doubled as a movie theatre for silent picture shows. Hosmer even had a red-light district.

However, the boom times were short-lived. In 1914, CPR closed the mine, disappointed with its production and unhappy with the difficulties and cost of extracting high-quality coal. Some miners moved to nearby Crowsnest Pass communities for work, while others signed up for military duty in the First World War. By the end of the summer of 1914, most of the mine's machinery had been shipped to other CPR coal-mining towns.

Charlie's family witnessed all the peaks and valleys of Hosmer's fortunes before the first coal was shipped out. On August 1, 1908, for example, thousands of Fernie citizens

—including Charlie's mother, Norma—were forced to flee the town when a huge bush fire advanced towards the downtown. Norma was only six years old. She was with her mother, Drucella Dubois, when a neighbour knocked on their door and told them everybody had to evacuate the town. Drucella hurriedly stuffed clothes and belongings in a satchel and grabbed Norma. They headed for the Crowsnest Pass Coal Company's office where hundreds of panic-stricken people were congregating. The building was already smouldering from the intense heat, and they could see flames shooting up in the air just a block away.

Drucella heard a rumour that a train was leaving the stricken city from the Western Canada Wholesalers warehouse, heading east on the CPR line. She and Norma rushed through the heat and smoke to the building six blocks away. With the blaze rapidly advancing, the train's engineer stayed until all hospital patients were boarded, as well as the women and children, who were wrapped in wet blankets by nurses and volunteers.

The train left at 3 p.m., but didn't get to Hosmer until five hours later. Along the way, the fire raced ahead of the train, destroying and knocking down trees on the rail tracks as it went. Several times the train had to stop so that crew members could leap off and remove the blazing debris. Throughout the ordeal, the engineer feared a derailment, which would mean almost certain death for everyone on board. When the train finally arrived at Hosmer, officials sent the evacuees to the mine's coke-oven complex, which was not yet operating. If the heat became too intense, officials added, they should "brick themselves in." Every one of the mine's 240 ovens was soon occupied.

Fortunately, the fire bypassed Hosmer. The only damage resulted when the mine's powder magazine exploded, shattering every window in town. The evacuees watched the fire while sipping tea made from water extracted from the train locomotive's boiler.

Meanwhile, Norma's father, who was left behind in Fernie, walked the rail line to Hosmer. He arrived hours later in the dead of night. "My mother had put me to bed in a coke oven wearing my winter coat, which I still have," Norma recounted several years later. "I woke up sometime in the night and my father was there. I couldn't figure out how he'd gotten there."

Norma and her family returned to Fernie on August 2 to find the town nearly levelled. The fire killed 10 residents, destroyed more than 1,000 buildings, and left 6,000 people homeless.

The coke-oven experience was the beginning of the family's long history in Hosmer. When Norma was expecting Charlie in 1920, she tried to hire a local midwife, as doctors declined going to Hosmer because of its isolation. Shortly before Charlie was due, the midwife excused herself after going on a drinking binge. Norma was left no other option but to take the eastbound train to Coleman, Alberta, where

Charlie was born on October 8. She took him back to Hosmer 10 days later.

By 1920, much of Hosmer was already torn down, and many residences had been dismantled and shipped to Coleman for incoming miners and their families. Times in Hosmer were wretched for most people. Some residents even burned down their homes to collect the insurance money.

Nevertheless, Charlie's family stayed. For a while his grandfather, Frank Dubois, ran a paper mill and his dad, Franklin Fink, became the janitor at the local school. Franklin also trapped and raised honeybees. Norma helped Drucella at the post office.

For more than 50 years, Charlie worked in the lumber and logging camps throughout the rugged mountain region. When he was laid off, he either trapped to make ends meet or headed back to Hosmer, his lifelong home base. Whenever he returned, he always lived in the family home, originally built in 1910 and purchased by his father in 1927. Over seven decades later, Charlie still had the same arm-chair his parents used—complete with the bullet hole left by an irate school trustee who stormed the house one night in 1932 to shoot his grandfather.

Frank Dubois, a past secretary with the local school, had learned that the new secretary was helping herself to school funds. In an effort to cover her tracks, she gave about $200 to one of the school's trustees who agreed to hold on to the money. Both of them started to panic and word began spreading around town. The trustee was convinced he was going to get blamed, caught by police and thrown in jail. Frank, he surmised, could prove who took the money and would likely be the one to turn him in.

In a rattled state, the trustee went to Frank's house with a rifle and fired it through the front door. Luckily, Frank saw the shadow of his would-be shooter outside the window and ducked quickly to one side. He was grazed by the bullet, which continued on, passing through his wife's bedroom door and then through the wall, behind which slept his daughter, Drucella. The bullet was later found six metres from the house, by the woodshed door, and the jacket of the bullet was found in the armchair—where it remains lodged to this day.

The shooter took off, running across the nearby creek and up to the local hotel, hoping to get a stiff drink to calm his shaken nerves. But there was worse trouble to come. "He had a hassle up there with the old owner of the hotel and his nephew. He wanted beer, but it was a Sunday and the owner wouldn't sell it to him," says Charlie. "So, he pulled out a knife. I know the nephew got cut, but they did manage finally to get the knife away from him." The police were called, but the disgraced trustee was never found or heard from again.

Charlie retired from driving in 2001 after 61 years on the road. He stays pretty much at home, chopping wood alongside his dog, Charlie. Sometimes he takes a walk up to the hotel, where he regales locals with many of his stories over a coffee. There isn't much left of the original townsite in Hosmer. Part of the foundation of the old bank lies near the highway, and of course there's Charlie's house. Across town over the rail tracks and up a mountain road is the pioneer cemetery, the final resting place of "Hosmer Hero" Fred Alderson, a mine rescue team member who died while trying to save workers in the Bellevue, Alberta, coal-mine disaster in 1910. Although many miners got out alive, 30 others were lost, including Alderson. Lower down the mountainside from the cemetery are the coke ovens. Not far from those are the magnificent tipple ruins, and farther along an overgrown trail across Hosmer Creek are the haunting concrete skeletons of the mine's boiler and powerhouses. Over the years, Hosmer locals have worked tirelessly to have all these relics preserved for future generations. It's been an uphill battle.

In the meantime, Charlie keeps the tales alive.

"It isn't the telling of the history, it's the people. It isn't the buildings or the structures. They're just part of the weave," says Fred Lightfoot, a Hosmer historian. "What really counts are the people, the hardships that they went through, the struggles. Charlie is one of those: quite a character, quite a story."

Bad Blood

WATER FROM THE KOOCANUSA RIVER gushed into the pastoral Waldo valley, obliterating farms and ranches, hopes and dreams. The flood marked the end of a bitter struggle that former residents of the area will never forget.

These former Waldo residents still talk about those painful days in the early 1970s when, over a period of several years, their own government flooded the valley to create a reservoir, now known as Lake Koocanusa. They are still shaken by the memories of pensioners losing their homes, and of a diehard farmer who didn't leave until the water came creeping in under his door. They are still angry as they recall government actions that led to the destruction of their small community 50 kilometres southwest of Fernie.

Their troubles began in 1939, when it first became known that the Americans wanted to divert the Koocanusa River through their valley. The water was needed for a proposed dam in Libby, Montana, 110 kilometres to the south. Residents heard about the request, but few thought it would ever be granted. However, by the early 1960s, Canada had formally agreed. Despite residents' protests, their fate was sealed: everything they owned and had worked for would be swept away. The provincial government offered Waldo residents compensation for their land, but most residents considered the offers grossly unfair. By 1971, those residents who had refused to accept the offers began receiving expropriation notices. Long-held resentment against the government turned to rage.

Ed Fitzpatrick is one of the ranchers who was outraged by the "paltry" amount the government offered him for his land and by the finality of the expropriation notice: "It is essential that the clearing programme proceed as soon as possible. Although we trust that you will do nothing to impede the clearing process or take the law into your own hands, we are obliged to advise you that any obstruction will result in legal action being taken."

But Ed was not going to go down without a fight. He refused to let the bulldozers onto his land. His passionate defiance convinced the senior engineer on site not to proceed. However, the government was equally determined, and officials kept a close watch on Ed. While he was away from his ranch, government workers blockaded the road to his property. The bulldozers came in and all his remaining buildings were set on fire.

"What a shock it was when the neighbours told me," says Ed. "When I got back, the RCMP were there. They are the law. Eventually you take what they offer. There's nothing left to fight with."

Ernie Strauss, another long-time Waldo resident, lost 300 acres of land in the expropriation. However, he found a way to save at least some pieces of Waldo before government crews set fire to all the buildings. He salvaged some wooden rafters from the school where his wife had been a student and had later taught.

"I can show you the rafters of this old building out in my yard," says Ernie. "I took a few rafters but the next day the official said that I couldn't take any more because a big CBC filming crew was coming to film the burning of the Waldo school." Ernie also hauled out an abandoned house, which he now uses as a garage and workshop. Another group of people saved Waldo's non-denominational church by moving it to Baynes Lake, a community two kilometres northeast of Waldo that many former Waldo residents now call home.

Lorraine Palmer, whose family had lived in Waldo since the early 1900s, has her own bitter story of her fight to save her heritage. But she also has other stories of "bad blood" in Waldo.

Former Waldo resident Ernie Strauss in front of Lake Koocanusa. Waldo now lies beneath the reservoir.

Lorraine's great-grandmother, Mary, had been running a boarding house in the coal-mining town of Coal Creek when she heard the Krag Hotel in Waldo was for sale. Being a smart businesswoman, she knew the Krag would be a viable business. Waldo was a new logging community and entrepreneurs already had plans in place to build sawmills. As well, Waldo was a stopping point for prospectors, trappers, loggers and lumberjacks whose lifestyles revolved around working in the bush and coming into town to unwind with hard liquor. Waldo's Krag Hotel was a popular stomping ground.

Since Mary was already accustomed to the rough and rowdy lifestyles of coal miners, she had few concerns about the hotel's clientele. She bought the hotel and moved to Waldo with her children.

The Palmers were proud of the Krag and ran it well. The two-storey hotel had a stately exterior with huge front porches stretching the width of the hotel on both floors. It had seven comfortable rooms for lodgers, a kitchen and a formal dining room, which Mary kept impeccable with clean tablecloths, fine china and sparkling cutlery. There was also a sitting room with its own stove and, of course, a bar.

Mary's son Billy, a former Coal Creek miner, was the Krag's manager. He was an amiable man, adept at handling his rowdy customers. He had been popular in Coal Creek and Fernie and was well liked in Waldo, too. Most of the Krag's customers were well-behaved, good old boys letting off steam after weeks of being isolated in the bush. Most—but not all.

One customer, Martin Haller, was a bit of a hermit. He lived in a cabin in the nearby Gold Creek area and subsisted mainly by hunting and trapping. He was overly fond of drinking and playing poker. Locals knew him to be a poor loser with a quick temper.

In the spring of 1910, Martin asked the Palmers for a job at the hotel. They hired him, but the 50-year-old proved to be unreliable, so Billy fired him and gave the job to another man, Bert Rawson. The Palmers soon learned that Martin was bitter about the dismissal and that he was becoming mentally unstable—a dangerous combination in a man who always carried his rifle.

One day during the early summer, Martin came to the Krag and hurled abuse at Billy and Bert. Billy told Martin to leave, but the angry man swore he would be back. For the next few weeks, he brooded about the perceived injustice. He threatened to kill both men and raze the hotel.

Constable William Leacy of the BC Provincial Police reported this threat to his superior and advised that Martin be taken into custody. Chief Sampson disregarded the suggestion.

During the evening of Saturday, August 20, Martin left his cabin and headed into Waldo, his rifle over his shoulder. Meanwhile, Mary and several hotel guests, including Constable Leacy, were eating supper in the dining room. On the other side of the hotel, Billy was tending bar.

Without warning, Martin burst into the bar, rifle in hand. He fixed Billy with a mad stare and yelled angrily. The noisy bar was suddenly silent. Horror-stricken, Billy ran for his own weapon. He snatched up his rifle and tried to take aim at his adversary, but Martin was already firing two rounds. Billy reeled, both hands clutching his chest. The bullets went straight through his body. One bullet passed completely through the outer wall of the hotel. The other lodged in the wall.

The two shots erupted like back-to-back explosions in the hotel. Mary and her dining-room guests rushed to the bar. Martin ordered them to go back, threatening to kill them if they came any closer. Mary ignored the threats and raced over to her stricken son.

Without a trace of emotion, Martin casually walked out of the bar and away from the hotel. No one dared to stop him as he headed off towards the Elk River. A doctor was called to the hotel, and then Billy was rushed to the hospital in Fernie. To his family's grief, the 32-year-old died from his wounds.

Constable Leacy contacted Chief Sampson in Fernie, and every available police officer was summoned to form a posse to apprehend Martin. The crazed gunman was seen by several people the next day, but nobody dared to approach him. The following day, Martin went back into Waldo and called in at the home of Peter Sandberg. The astonished man was well aware of the killer's deeds but had no way of calling the police. Luckily, patrons at the Krag Hotel saw the outlaw leave Sandberg's home and head down to the train station, still holding his rifle. They scurried inside the hotel and into the basement for cover. When the danger had passed, they contacted the police.

While police were racing to Waldo, Martin left the train station and began walking down a trail towards the bush. The police were soon closing in. Constable Leacy and two other members of the posse inched towards Martin. When the trio came within a few feet of him, the wild man fired two shots. No one was hit, but the men quickly retreated. Martin took off and ran back to the station. But the police were close behind and fired a fusillade of bullets at him as he crossed the tracks. The fugitive was hit. He staggered for an instant, but then gathered himself and continued running. Still clutching his rifle, he climbed a fence then dived into a small shack.

The posse followed cautiously, knowing he was injured and desperate. As the officers carefully approached the rear of the shack, one man crawled under a window and held a hat on a stick so that Martin could see it. The policemen cautiously worked their way around to the front of the house. As they inched closer, they realized further bloodshed was unnecessary. Martin lay sprawled on the porch in a pool of blood, seriously wounded but still alive. He looked up at his captors and gasped, "It's all over boys. I'm all in." He was arrested and taken to Fernie by train. The outlaw had lost a great deal of blood and eventually lapsed into a coma. He died early the next morning.

During the inquest, the jury was told that Constable Leacy had warned Chief Sampson that Martin was unstable and had made death threats. The jury ruled Martin was insane. It also ruled that a rigid inquiry be held into the negligence of Chief Sampson for not having Martin arrested and medically examined when he received Constable Leacy's report.

Later that week, Billy was buried in St. Margaret's Cemetery in Fernie. His obituary summed up the community's sense of loss. "The news of his untimely death has caused a pall of sadness to settle over many hearts. Billy, as he was familiarly known, was not considered of a disposition to provoke the enmity of any man."

For almost 20 years after Billy's murder, Waldo prospered as a community with a population of up to 200. However, a fire in 1929 destroyed the sawmill and other businesses. It was the beginning of the end of the community. The Depression had hit and the timber resources were diminishing, so business owners felt it was not worth rebuilding.

The Palmer family continued to operate the Krag Hotel until 1948, when dwindling business forced its permanent closure. For many years, the old hotel sat forlorn and boarded up, and then a few years before the area was flooded, the building burned to the ground. It was later learned that this was not an accident. It was another crime of revenge; another loss caused by "bad blood."

"It was done out of spite," says Lorraine. "Something to do with a killed dog in the Baynes Lake area. Somebody burned it down to get even."

Lorraine, Ed and Ernie have moved on with their lives. But it hasn't been easy. The painful memories are deeply ingrained. They still harbour a lot of hurt and resentment. Waldo, for better or worse, was their home. Once in a while they head down to the shore of Lake Koocanusa and look into the deep water. They see only drowned dreams and vanished hopes—and the anger of a community that still feels betrayed.

The Orchard

NOBBY HAYASHI AND HIS TEAMMATES were loaded up in the back of a truck. It was a balmy June afternoon in the summer of 1944, and they were off to play baseball. These high-spirited teenagers were the dazzling star players of The Orchard, the home of New Denver's brilliant baseball team.

It was a road game at Sandon, so they were facing a rough, hour-long ride from the valley into the mountains over 14 kilometres of steep, winding gravel road. But the boys didn't mind. They were just glad to be leaving their camp for the day. Still, the event was bittersweet.

Road games against a bunch of ballplayers from the ghost town of Sandon was not what Nobby had dreamed of before coming to the Slocan two years earlier. Back then, he had envisioned playing teams from towns and cities all along the West Coast—places that were bursting with excitement and civic pride. He had been a star Little League player in Little Tokyo, a Japanese-Canadian community in Vancouver. He was a power-hitting shortstop, climbing his way up the baseball ladder and hoping to play for the famed Asahi Baseball Club of Vancouver. The club had represented the city's Japanese-Canadian community since 1914, and the players thrilled fans at the Powell Street Grounds with their razzle-dazzle style of play. These players were heroes to all Japanese-Canadian children, especially to Nobby, who was the team's bat boy.

But in 1944, the most the 16-year-old could look forward to was an occasional outing to the neighbouring internment camp in Sandon, where almost 1,000 of his fellow Japanese-Canadians had been placed. As long as Canada was at war with Japan, playing his beloved baseball in the Valley of the Ghosts was as good as it would get. But it was better than nothing. It sustained him.

Six decades after that June day, Nobuyoshi Hayashi still remembers the emotions of the summer of 1944, the years that led to it and the years that followed. He still lives in New Denver and still goes by the name of Nobby, a nickname he was given while playing Little League. He is now a volunteer at the Nikkei Internment Centre, a memorial to the interned Japanese-Canadians. He greets visitors and tourists warmly. There is neither bitterness nor resentment at what he and his fellow Japanese-Canadians went through during the Second World War. He simply shares his memories.

One memory that is deeply ingrained is how his father, Tom, reacted to the government officials when they came to the Hayashi home with the dreaded "order" in 1942—the order that announced Japanese-Canadians were now "enemy aliens" and would be sent to internment camps for the duration of the war. Incredulous and angry, Tom stormed at the officials, "We fought for Canada and this is what we get?" The officials had no answer for him.

Tom had been in Canada since he was 15. Not only had he fought with the Canadian Army during the horrific First World War in France, he had proved himself to be a responsible, law-abiding citizen during the years that followed. He held a good job as a greeting host/chauffeur at the plush Hotel Vancouver, and he owned a comfortable home in Vancouver's Little Tokyo. Now his country was telling him that his loyalty was in doubt and that he and his family could not be trusted. He and his wife, Katsuko, were humiliated.

The Canadian government had made the decision to treat all Japanese-Canadians as aliens when the Japanese bombed the US naval base at Pearl Harbour, Hawaii. As part of the War Measures Act, the government passed an Order in Council giving the minister of justice the power to remove "any and all persons" from a designated protected zone. This protected zone included Vancouver and all other communities within 160 kilometres of the coast. For the thousands of Japanese-Canadians living in Vancouver and nearby communities, this meant being forcibly moved to relocation camps outside that zone.

On March 4, 1942, the BC Security Commission was established, and 22,000 Japanese-Canadians were given 24 hours to pack before being incarcerated and interned. The government confiscated everything Tom and his family owned: their home, vehicle, bank accounts and even their Canadian naturalization papers. Like thousands of other Japanese-Canadians, they had to hand over their belongings and possessions to the Custodian of Enemy Alien Property as a "protective measure only." All they were allowed to take with them was 69 kilograms of luggage for each adult, and 23 kilograms for each child. "We didn't know what to pack because we didn't know what was going on or where we were going to," says Nobby.

Hundreds of families were assembled in Vancouver's Hastings Park, where they were herded into animal stalls before being shipped out to the BC interior. Their destinations were wilderness "relocation camps" or sugar-beet farms in Alberta, Manitoba and Ontario. Nobby and his family were to be sent to the Slocan, a former silver-mining boom area in British Columbia's West Kootenay region.

Canadian government officials separated most adult men from the ages of 18 to 45 from their families to work on road projects in the wilderness. Because Tom was 47,

Nobby's family was spared that heartbreak. They would be living in the same camp, even though he would not be allowed to live in the same dwelling as his family for some time. Tom, along with a group of other men, was sent to New Denver to help set up the camp before the women and children arrived. Later, because he was a war veteran, he was given a job as an interpreter.

Nobby still remembers that first journey from Vancouver with his mother and siblings. "In the passenger train, we had a seat you could turn into a bed. Food was delivered to each train car. You ate right there and slept right there. You couldn't get out."

They were one of the first families to arrive in New Denver, a small town located along the eastern shore of Slocan Lake, a 40-kilometre waterway that runs between the Valhalla Mountains and the Selkirk Mountains.

New Denver was already a town with a history. A camp had been settled there in 1890, when prospectors first came with dreams of silver riches. It was originally named Eldorado, but later changed to New Denver after Denver, Colorado. By 1893, the town became a major supply centre for the "Silvery Slocan" communities and camps, as well as an important port. Like other boomtowns, however, New Denver's fortunes had sagged by the late 1920s.

By 1942, New Denver was a community fast becoming another one of the Slocan's ghost towns. As tragic as the internment camps were, many remaining locals welcomed the internees, hoping they would breathe new life and hope into the declining region.

There were only a few dozen people still living in New Denver at that time, the majority being older adults. Most of the young men had already enlisted in the military, and the young women had left the gloom for larger and more promising urban centres. The sight of the boarded-up stores and burned shells of houses made the new arrivals think they were coming to a doomed community. It did nothing to alleviate their sense of despair.

New Denver witnessed the influx of 1,400 Japanese-Canadians. In all, about 12,000 arrived in the Slocan region, more than half of the total 22,000 Japanese-Canadians interned across the country during the Second World War. Besides New Denver and Sandon, other Slocan Valley camps included Greenwood, Salmo, Rosebery, Lemon Creek, Slocan City and Kaslo. Each of these locations has interesting histories, but Sandon is the most well known today.

At the turn of the 20th century, Sandon became the most famous and prosperous silver-mining community in Canadian history. John Morgan Harris, a local entrepreneur, led the town to a period of prosperity that caught the imagination of the world mining community. It was a wild, wilderness locale that boasted almost 5,000 silver-hungry citizens, 29 hotels, 28 saloons and up to 50 brothels in the young city's notorious red-light district. But fires, strikes and plummeting world silver prices doomed Sandon's fortunes, and by 1942 only 50 hearty souls remained.

The internees swelled the population by 953. They moved into the dozens of abandoned and derelict buildings, and children played on the ski-jump hill and in the abandoned sports and recreational facilities. Despite the relative freedom, the newcomers never forgot they were prisoners. The living conditions were harsh, especially during the bitterly cold winters. Many remember Sandon as "Camp Hell-Hole."

New Denver's Japanese-Canadians did not fare any better. Their new home on the shores of Slocan Lake was far more scenic—and warmer—than Sandon. But the camp was completely fenced and was further separated from the town on its north side by Carpenter Creek. It had the deceptively charming name of The Orchard because the land, the 80-acre Harris Ranch, was covered with ancient apple trees. Most of the trees were either dead or dying, so were cleared and eventually used to construct the internment houses. This green timber was an unsatisfactory building material. It shrank, creating gaps that let in the cold air and rain.

When Nobby and his family arrived in 1942, the houses were not ready. For the first year, families had to live in tepee-style army surplus tents and share outhouses with other families. Nobby, his mother and seven siblings crammed into their tiny tent. They slept in four beds, three of them double bunks. Each person was given two blankets. When the winter came, mothers packed their children four to a bed to keep warm.

Eventually, 124 two-family and 24 single-family dwellings were built. These dwellings housed 1,016 people—an average of seven people per house. The single-family units were four and a half metres by six metres, and two-family homes measured four and a half metres by nine metres. Each dwelling was equipped with heaters, cookstoves, wooden sinks and straw mattresses. There were no ceilings and no insulation. The roofs were covered with tarpaper until better material was available. When electricity was finally supplied to The Orchard in the spring of 1943, families were given one 25-watt bulb for each room. Before that, the shabby dwellings had been lit by candles and coal lamps.

Six months after Katsuko and the children moved into their home, Tom was allowed to join them. Finally all the homes had been built, and the following year the construction crews built a school and a community hall. Much to the joy of Nobby and the other boys, the men also constructed a baseball diamond.

Until 1943, the residents of The Orchard were not allowed into New Denver's downtown unless they had to shop. At first, the locals were suspicious and even paranoid. Marguerite Campbell, a New Denver resident who was 17 when the Japanese-Canadians arrived, remembers it well. "I know one of the local ladies was sure she was going to be stabbed in her bed but there was nothing to indicate that,"

Nobby Hayashi swings while playing for the
Vernon Blues in 1948.

she says. Marguerite and the other few remaining young
women were pleased about the sudden influx of young men.
"We found that they were just like us. They liked Glenn
Miller records, and Tommy Dorsey. We never felt afraid."

Marguerite became aware of the action on The Orchard
ball diamond, where the young, handsome Japanese-
Canadian men turned heads and played superlative
baseball. She particularly recalls Nobby, the hot-hitting

shortstop and catcher who was becoming well known in the area. After the war, Marguerite's husband coached Nobby.

By 1943, the Japanese-Canadians had made a positive financial impact on New Denver. Marguerite's parents were one couple whose business benefited from their presence. They owned a dairy, and during that first year, they had about 1,000 new customers. The dairy was so busy, Marguerite's parents expanded it and had to hire more staff. Since Caucasian locals were in short supply, young Japanese-Canadians were hired instead.

"They were treated well, the ones who worked for my parents," says Marguerite. "They bottled milk and sold it, and my father delivered it to The Orchard. In the wintertime when the snow got too high, he took horses and a wagon. Little kids ran behind the horses, and he let them ride in the back of the wagon. In my home, they were people just like anybody else who happened to come to New Denver."

By the spring of 1943, Nobby was already playing baseball again. His lifelong passion for the game had not been dulled by his shattering experiences. Like the other young players in the other camps, he still wanted to improve his skills and do what he loved best. Baseball was more than just a game—it helped them survive those years of broken dreams.

"You didn't think of anything else, especially all that you had lost," says Nobby. "Some people still have it in their minds, what they lost and never got anything back for it. Some people carried it until they died."

Caucasian sports fans who were able—and willing—to watch the Japanese-Canadian players were surprised and impressed with the quality of play. Nobby, especially, caused a stir. Towards the end of the war, a fellow Slocan Valley internee who was coaching the players told Nobby he could become a quality catcher. Nobby was a special baseball commodity in that he was a power hitter who could also hit for average.

Life had settled into a routine for Nobby and his family when they were hit with another tragedy. Tom had a heart attack and died in the spring of 1945, just a few short months before the end of the war. Katsuko and her children were devastated. Tom's untimely death cast a deep shadow over the relief they felt on hearing the war had ended.

Although Canada was no longer at war with Japan, Japanese-Canadians could not go back to within 160 kilometres of the West Coast. Nor could they reclaim the property that had been held "in trust" by the Custodian of Enemy Property. Everything they owned had been sold, without their consent, to pay for their living expenses during the internment.

Life did not get any better for Katsuko and her family during the next few years. In fact, without Tom to fend for them, it got worse. Although they were no longer locked inside The Orchard, they stayed because they had nowhere else to go. Like other mothers, Katsuko continued to live in her shack and raise her family as best she could on the $50 a month government allowance.

Nobby, being the oldest son, now had to find work to help support his family. As soon as travel restrictions eased, he was able to go the Okanagan region of the BC interior to pick apples. He was soon playing baseball again, and scouts noticed him immediately.

"My average was between .385 and .400." says Nobby. "I had a chance of making it." By the spring of 1946, he got a tryout call from the Portland Beavers in Oregon, a Triple A–level farm team of the major league Brooklyn Dodgers. He made the team and was also able to get a day job to earn extra money to send back to his family in The Orchard.

Nobby never did get the call to go to the "Big Show," but he continued to excel at the minor professional level, hitting around .350 in the two years he played in Portland. An injury in 1948 forced him to take some time off, so he returned to New Denver to visit his family. By this time, most residents had rebuilt simple houses on the sites of their shacks, and their lives regained some normalcy.

Nobby didn't return to Portland after the injury healed. Instead, he went back to the Okanagan because he wanted to be closer to "home." Despite the daunting memories New Denver held for Nobby and his family, it had become their home.

After three seasons with the Vernon Blues, Nobby went

back to New Denver, hoping to find a job. But steady work was scarce in the area, so he went off to play ball once again. This time he went to Lethbridge, Alberta, where he played four seasons with another Brooklyn Dodgers farm club and helped them win a southern Alberta championship. During these years, he also worked at a local cannery to supplement his income.

After the 1955 season, Nobby came home for good. He was now 27 and ready to settle down. He felt he had given his best to the game and was happy to "retire." He worked at a nearby sawmill and later found another job in the logging industry. Nobby got married in 1957, the year The Orchard was closed as a camp.

The provincial government divided the former internment camp into 13.5 metre by 30 metre residential lots and gave residents the deeds. Katsuko lived there until her death in 1974.

Nobby remained in New Denver and worked for the BC government in the highways and transportation department until his retirement in 1988. This was a banner year for Japanese-Canadians—the Canadian government finally recognized its responsibility for the plight of Japanese-Canadians during the Second World War.

On September 22, 1988, Prime Minister Brian Mulroney, on behalf of the Government of Canada, offered a formal apology to Japanese-Canadians for the injustices committed against them. A redress settlement was also announced, which included individual financial compensation for all survivors. Nobby was awarded $21,000. "It took them 40 years. It wasn't Mulroney's fault. It was the governments before him. It was better to accept it than not to," he says.

The memories of the tragic years in New Denver inspired Nobby and fellow members of the Kyowakai Society—the last internment camp organization in existence—to build a permanent memorial to the interned Japanese-Canadians. "We thought we should have a memorial somewhere because all of the other camps are buried and have disappeared," says Nobby. "This is to remind everybody and hope that it doesn't happen to anybody else."

The Nikkei Internment Memorial Centre was built at a cost of $500,000—half of which was paid by the federal government. It first opened its doors to the general public in July of 1994. It sits on a parcel of land where The Orchard's original community centre still stands. As well as the centre, the site displays three original internment shacks. The buildings are set in a memorial garden designed by a Japanese gardener who was interned in the area.

New Denver has rebounded to a village of 600 citizens. The community is an eclectic mix of artisans, small-business people, environmentalists, loggers and tourism operators. It is popular with tourists for its natural beauty and leisurely pace. It has fared far better than the other Valley of the Ghost communities. Although Sandon is famous and attracts thousands of visitors, it will always be a sad ghost town that will never again feel the heartbeat of a vibrant community.

Nobby now lives in the home once owned by his mother. Despite the challenges and hardships he has endured, he has lived a full and rewarding life. He has achieved many of his goals, both in baseball and in his personal life. This gracious man feels the past sadness and tragedy of The Orchard was in another time and place. He will never forget it, but neither will he harbour ill will.

PHOENIX

Ghost City

FROM THEIR PERCH IN THE back of the family sleigh, six-year-old Bob Forshaw and his younger brother, Jim, looked back towards Phoenix, the city where they had been born. Sad and confused, the boys wondered why they were leaving their home. They couldn't figure it out, but they knew something was up. The sleigh was packed with all the family's possessions, even the piano.

Their parents couldn't explain they were leaving because the self-proclaimed "highest city in Canada," a once-booming copper-mining community 1,412 metres above sea level, had become the country's highest ghost city. They sat quietly up front, braving the cold night air of January 1, 1920. The sleigh moved slowly down the snowy, winding road, taking them to their new home in Greenwood, another community in the Boundary Country, eight kilometres from Phoenix.

It was several years before Bob and Jim really understood. But they never forgot the sense of sadness that had touched them—and many others—when they left their copper-mountain home.

The Forshaws often went back to Phoenix to look around. Each time they went, the former copper city of Canada looked more forlorn and derelict. It was hard for them to imagine this was the same place that once bustled with 4,000 copper-crazy citizens and boasted 20 hotels and saloons, gambling casinos, four churches, an impressive city hall, a covered skating rink, hospital, brewery, an electric power company, telephone exchanges and even an opera house.

As they roamed around, Robert Forshaw, the boys' father, told them that Phoenix had been well known for its sports teams. In 1911, Phoenix's hockey team won the provincial championship. That same year, they asked for the right to challenge for the Stanley Cup—professional hockey's biggest prize. Unfortunately, they were too late to qualify. As well, according to some locals, Phoenix had British Columbia's first women's hockey team, which advertised itself as "the world's first skirt and leg exhibition."

Bob, a retired university professor who now lives in nearby Grand Forks, says Phoenix was a magical place for children to play. He and Jim used to race through entire streets of empty buildings, all boarded up and ghostly.

They would dart from one house to another, exploring the rooms and exclaiming over their amazing finds. "There were some homes where people just left the kitchenware right on the table and left," says Bob. "They got no help in moving or anything."

This is testimony to how quickly the city emptied after the mine owners—the Granby Company—loaded the last pioneer-era trainload of ore on June 14, 1919. That load ended a wild and memorable era in Canadian mining history that began in 1891 and produced 13,678,901 tons of ore. Many of the miners and their families left that night to look for new jobs at other mining locales. It was the beginning of the exodus.

Robert was not a miner, so he did not have to abandon his home hastily to beat the rush for jobs in the other mines. He was a "jack of all trades" and had been since he first arrived in Phoenix in 1907. After marrying in 1913, he bought a 20-acre ranch two kilometres from Phoenix for $8,000. From there, he wholesaled anything he could lay his hands on, including wood and coal. Robert also prospected and worked at odd jobs for the mine. Some of those jobs were more "odd" than others. Two were downright unenviable: cleaning the town's outhouses and digging graves.

"Dad and Uncle Walter had to go out to the outhouses after midnight. The word honey wagon came to be," says Bob. "There were no flush toilets in those days. They emptied them once a month, bringing it down to our ranch and plowing it under. One lady told me about hearing the wagon grinding over the rocks one night and one of the hind wheels fell off. A lot of the contents came out over my dad. He stood there in the calm of the night, about two or three in the morning and shouted, 'Shit, shit, nothing but shit.'"

The other task, digging graves, was more grisly and potentially more dangerous—especially during the Spanish flu epidemic of 1918, which claimed dozens of lives in Phoenix. "About half the graves in the cemetery are due to death because of the flu, young folks in particular," says Bob. "Dad was kept busy from morning until night digging graves, by hand in those days. Mother thought he would get the flu, but he never did."

After moving to Greenwood, Robert received permission from the provincial government to sell vacant Phoenix homes for $5 and $10, depending on the size. Bob and Jim tagged along on these excursions, relishing the chance to play in the ghost city. They also hunted gophers, played in the cemetery and gathered copper wire for their dad.

As the wilderness began to reclaim Phoenix, wild mushrooms flourished, especially during the fall rainy season. "The electric light poles were falling down in those days," says Bob. "Some of the mushrooms would be so thick that they would actually lift the poles off the ground." That's when the Forshaws took along a frying pan and made themselves delicious lunches.

The fun-loving family was not quite alone during its

visits to the ghost city. A trio of legendary bachelors still lived there. They were the eccentric William Bambury, the American prospector Bob Denzler and an unforgettable fellow by the name of Adolph Sercu, better known to Boundary Country folks as Forepaw.

"They kept to themselves," says Bob. "I knew them well. They were all very decent to me and were very fine people. Each was different."

Denzler, who arrived in the area in 1891, is credited with one of the first major copper discoveries for Phoenix mines. This discovery triggered an onslaught of claims. Soon, a settlement called Greenwood Camp had been established. When the first post office opened on October 1, 1898, the name was officially changed to Phoenix.

Denzler became wealthy. Although he was an American citizen and kept a home in Spokane, Washington, he spent the summers in Phoenix—even after the mine closed. "He was supposed to have made a find which he covered up so that no one else could find it," says Bob. "But unfortunately, nor could he! He kept coming back year after year, until he was too old, to see if he could find the mine. But he never did."

Although the trio kept to themselves in the ghost city, once in a while their paths crossed in the empty streets. Also, apparently, they exchanged magazines and other reading material. One such trade caused Denzler great embarrassment while American guests were staying at his house. The visit had gone well until the ladies started reading some of Denzler's magazines. Turning to a page that displayed an ad for fingernail polish, they were horrified to find their host had written terrible things in the margins. Unbeknown to Denzler, Bambury had written: "Typical American hussies, white cockroaches I call them." When the women confronted Denzler with the magazine, the poor man was aghast. Luckily, the ladies accepted his explanation that the messages were written by Bambury. The gentlemanly Denzler assured them that, although he had some strange ways, his neighbour was a decent man.

Bambury was an Englishman who had come to Canada in 1887. After spending several years in Nelson, BC, trying to make a go of a boat-repair business, he came to Phoenix in either 1900 or 1902. His life during the boom times of Phoenix is a mystery to old-timers, but Bambury certainly became a legend after Phoenix became the ghost city of the Boundary.

For years, he lived tax- and rent-free in the former home of Dr. Boucher. While Denzler was renowned for keeping his house immaculately clean, Bambury was notorious for his lack of housekeeping skills. "He lived like a hermit. His place was filthy, but interesting," says Bob.

Bambury read voraciously, and there were always stacks of books, newspapers and magazines in his house. As well as scrawling comments in magazines, he also wrote copiously in his private journals. He wrote about his unique lifestyle in the ghost city. One entry in his diary reads, "Kept a fire in the bedroom all night with no entirely satisfactory results altho' no ice formed in the room. It was no different in the other bedroom, where I had to use an axe in the bathtub before I could take my bath."

Bambury eked out a living in the ghost town by salvaging lumber and metal. Also, he sometimes got the odd maintenance job along the highway outside Greenwood.

Although he spent most of his time alone, he was never known to be shy when he needed a good home-cooked meal. Many times he walked the eight kilometres to Greenwood for a hot supper at the Forshaw residence. Bob recalls one of his visits. "He once came to our place and he told Mother, 'Today is Queen Maude of Norway's birthday.' I don't know if there was a Queen Maude or not. He would tell Mother how he lived on two peanuts a day. He joined us for supper, and I remember once we had chicken pot pie. He ate about half of it."

When the meal was over, Bambury usually buried himself in a book or magazine. When it got late, Bob's parents would go to bed, leaving their guest to his reading. They never asked him stay. Sometime during the early hours of the morning, Bambury would bundle himself up and trudge back to his beloved ghost city.

As eccentric as Bambury was, some Boundary Country old-timers say he was not quite as peculiar as the last of the trio, Adolph Sercu. Forepaw, as Sercu called himself, was Belgian. He had gone to the United States in the 1890s and

Adolph "Forepaw" Sercu in the abandoned city of Phoenix in the 1930s with his crop of salad grown from Belgian seed.

then came up to Phoenix shortly before the turn of the 20th century. Among other things he was also a prospector and found a claim near the city in 1900.

"He was a hard worker. He used to have cattle, and he would drive them to Greenwood. He had a garden down near Boundary Creek. He always had this rifle with him, which usually was under the seat of the democrat," says Bob.

"One morning at about four thirty or five o'clock, he was leaving to go to work and he threw the gun in the democrat. He had his hand over the muzzle and the safety catch must have caught on a nail and went off. He phoned us and asked me if my daddy could come and get him because he blew his hand off. He was taken to Grand Forks hospital and they removed the hand and left him with a stub."

Forepaw, or "4 Paw" as he signed himself, later had a blacksmith fashion an iron hook onto his arm, but it didn't stop him from trying to be a sure-shot marksman. One time on a buggy trip with Bob, Forepaw pulled out his rifle to shoot one of his steers. Unfortunately, he missed. He killed a prized blue heifer instead.

Forepaw, for better or worse, felt a serious kinship with guns. When Phoenix became a ghost town, a fund was set up to appoint a watchman to guard against scavengers and vandals. Forepaw enthusiastically accepted the role. He moved right into the still-stately city hall, where he set himself up as mayor, chief of police and magistrate. Forepaw was determined to earn his keep and made it known to all ghost-city visitors that he was the law. It was also clear to many former residents that Forepaw wanted to continue the legacy of Phoenix's colourful magistrate, Judge Willie Williams. This old character became known for his booming declaration, "I am the highest judge, in the highest court, in the highest city in Canada."

Forepaw wanted his authority established beyond a

Phoenix's First World War cenotaph, built in the early years of the 20th century, is the only reminder from the city's glory days still standing on the site of the former copper-mining community.

doubt. He walked the deserted streets with a billy club in his hand and a homemade badge on his chest—a star he had cut from a tin can. The self-proclaimed lawman was always on the lookout for "undesirables"—he even found a few.

"During the Depression, people used to go up to Phoenix to see what they could pick up. Dad was camping and prospecting in Phoenix, and he and Forepaw saw two men and went up to the house where they had left their bikes. As they were going by, Dad grabbed one and held him while Forepaw grabbed the other. He got away; so then Forepaw went blazing after him with a gun. I remember they took him down and locked him in the old jail overnight. Forepaw wouldn't give him back his bike for the longest time."

One by one, Phoenix's last trio of residents passed on. Forepaw passed away in 1942. His death was front-page news in the *Grand Forks Gazette* with a headline reading: THE MAYOR AND HOST OF PHOENIX HAS GIVEN LAST WELCOME TO FAMOUS CAMP. His remains were laid to rest in the old Phoenix cemetery. Later, locals discovered that Forepaw had lost a huge estate inheritance to the German Nazis when Hitler invaded Belgium in 1940. Forepaw had given little thought to it. He told friends he would rather have "peace in Phoenix than a dazzling fortune in Belgium under rule of Hitler."

Denzler died in 1944, so Bambury was left alone to watch over Phoenix. In late 1949, the 82-year-old grudgingly conceded that he could no longer survive the Phoenix winters. He rented a room at Greenwood's Windsor Hotel. There, he continued to write his diaries and even itemized all the possessions he had taken with him to Greenwood. They included a dictionary, a copy of *Maclean's* magazine and a Bible map.

The following May, Bambury returned to Phoenix for

the summer, and perhaps for the first and only time, he noticed how much the city he adored had deteriorated. In a diary entry of May 28, 1950, he wrote, "In strolling around this morning I observed that the wreckage of the King's Hotel with that of the Belleville Hotel seems to have sunk considerably, giving the impression that a mine cave-in has caused the subsidence. Water not far below, apparently."

Phoenix's last resident died in December 1951. He was laid to rest in the old cemetery. Phoenix was now alone with the ghosts.

But Phoenix did rise again—as an open-pit mining venture in the 1950s. The mine operated on and off until 1978, but the company was not interested in making the old buildings habitable. Sadly, they were all bulldozed and buried. Today, all that remains of Phoenix is a gigantic open-pit mining scar, the pioneer cemetery and—outside the former city limits—a First World War cenotaph.

A more modern reminder of the city is displayed in downtown Greenwood: a metal sculpture of a phoenix created by miners in the 1970s. People of the Boundary Country know that the city has as much chance of rising again as the commemorative sculpture. Some, like Bob Forshaw, wish it had never been allowed to die. "It was a pity that we didn't preserve it," says Bob. "Had it been preserved, we would have knocked the socks off of Barkerville!"

Uninvited Guests

THE BUSH PILOT WOKE FROM a deep sleep and peered into the darkness of the hotel room. A shape emerged from the shadows—a woman's shape—and she was sitting at the end of his bed. Before the startled man could collect his thoughts, she had melted away.

Krystyna Plewinski and Keith Thomas, owners of Trout Lake's historic Windsor Hotel, smile as they recall their guest's nocturnal surprise. When he checked in, he had told Krystyna he did not believe the stories of the Trout Lake ghosts. But he checked out first thing the next morning, swearing he had seen one of them.

Trout Lake, a once-booming gold- and silver-mining town, is now a community of 26 people—retirees, provincial road workers and those like Krystyna and Keith who are in the tourist trade. This almost abandoned town in southern British Columbia's Lardeau Country qualifies as a ghost town, as it is a mere shadow of the "city" it once was. There are scores of such ghost towns scattered throughout British Columbia—but they don't all have their own ghosts.

A famous ghost town about 400 kilometres to the north-west, Barkerville, has its share of phantoms. But while the custodians of Barkerville don't know who those northern spectres are—or were—some Trout Lake residents are pretty sure one of their ghosts is Mrs. Alice Jowett, the Grand Old Lady of the Lardeau.

Alice, a refined Englishwoman, came to Trout Lake City in 1896 during the boom times. An energetic woman in her early 40s, she began looking for a business venture. She purchased the Trout Lake City Hotel and ran it successfully, catering to miners and loggers. In 1907, she sold the hotel and purchased the much larger Windsor Hotel. Here, she established a reputation as the most respected proprietor in the Lardeau.

Perhaps because of her English background, Alice always insisted on a high level of decorum. Very few people ever addressed her by anything other than Mrs. Jowett. She also insisted on a high standard of service. Even as Trout Lake City slid into decline in the early 1930s, she made sure the dining-room tables were set with the best linens, silver and crystal.

Alice took great pride in the hotel, but it wasn't her only interest. She became a passionate prospector. According to Edna Daney, a long-time Trout Lake resident who worked for Alice in the early 1930s, the elegant woman was never happier than when she was prospecting—or talking about it.

There was little time for idle chatter between Alice and her 17-year-old employee. They rose early and plunged into the daily chores together, not pausing until 11 a.m., when Alice would stop whatever she was doing to down her daily shot of brandy. But whenever they did talk, it was about mining.

"That was all she would talk about if you'd let her," says 90-year-old Edna. "In later years she had the Foggy Day Mine and always thought that it would be the mine of the country, but it never turned out that way. Everybody seemed to accept her as a mining woman," adds Edna. "All the engineers would come in and they all knew her and treated her as an equal person."

Over the years, Alice accumulated dozens of gold- and silver-mining claims, but the Foggy Day was her favourite. She loved assessing these claims herself and would regularly hike up to the sites to collect assay samples. Although a congenial woman, well liked by her staff and hotel guests, her quick temper erupted whenever men tried to help her with the assessments or any other mining tasks. She left her would-be helpers with no doubt that she was thoroughly capable of doing everything herself. Doubtless, some of these men shook their heads as they watched the sturdy, white-haired woman heading up the trails, prospector's pick in hand, but they didn't offer help or advice again.

Alice spent as much time at the Foggy Day mine as she could. In later years, she had a cabin built in the alpine meadow below the mine so she could stay overnight in comfort. "In the middle of the afternoon she would decide that she had to go up there, and she'd get someone to row her eight miles down the lake and up to the alpine basin," says Edna, who later married Alice's grandson Seldon. "My husband used to take groceries in to her, and he would go up once in awhile and look after the horses."

Although Alice never made her fortune from her claims, she never lost her enthusiasm for prospecting. In 1945, at the age of 92, she sold the hotel. When she died 10 years later, family and friends built a cairn in her memory. It stands in the meadow, below the Foggy Day mine.

During the three decades after Alice's retirement, the Windsor Hotel changed hands several times. Due to neglect, it fell into disrepair—as did many of the abandoned homes in the gradually emptying town. Since 1994, however, the three-storey, wooden frame hotel has been rejuvenated. Keith and Krystyna restored the hotel and furnished most of the rooms with period and original pieces. The Grand Old Lady of the Lardeau would have found these rooms very familiar and inviting—perhaps too inviting.

Krystyna said the reports of a ghost at the Windsor Hotel began five years before they moved in. She said a cook who

Barkerville's Main Street today. With just a handful of people living in the Cariboo Gold Rush community in the late 1950s, it has rebounded to become a major heritage town and tourist attraction.

had worked at the hotel in the early 1980s swears she encountered Alice, and that the phantom even greeted her. She described the apparition as a sturdily built, white-haired woman with an easy smile.

Krystyna has never seen the phantom, but she did witness an eerie event. "One of my housekeepers once lost a key," she says. "We looked through everything for it and then it just fell from the sky in front of her as she was walking up the stairs. I saw it happen. I heard the clink, and there it was."

Edna steadfastly refuses to believe the hotel is haunted. "Bah! There are no ghosts at the Windsor," she says firmly. "I often wondered what they had been drinking that made them say they saw ghosts. If Mrs. Jowett was alive today, she'd say fiddle-dee-dee to that idea!"

However, Krystyna and Keith say they get about one report of a sighting every year from their guests. But these sightings are not all of a white-haired woman. Many are of a "dark-haired lady." Four of the most credible reports have come from children—individually, not collectively. They claim to have seen the woman in their bedrooms.

"There would be no reason for them to lie or even know about the ghost," says Krystyna. "The sightings usually occur when the parents go down to the bar after they have put their children to bed. The child will come down and say some dark-haired lady was upstairs and told them to go downstairs. There was nobody upstairs," Krystyna adds emphatically, "and they don't say 'ghost,' they just say 'dark-haired lady.'"

Some ghost-story enthusiasts suggest both the apparitions are Alice, but at different stages in her earthly life. But, whether or not the two Windsor Hotel phantoms are one and the same, they are both dignified and decorous, as Mrs. Jowett had been. The Barkerville ghost, on the other hand, is neither. She is cheeky—always appearing in her nightgown—and mischievous. In short, she reflects the spirit of Barkerville, the rip-roaring centre of the mid-1800s Cariboo Gold Rush.

One could speculate she was one of the lost loves of Billy Barker (the irascible 19th-century Englishman who gave Barkerville its name), or a madam from one of the many bawdy houses that prospered in British Columbia's interior in those days. But whoever she is, there are no known reports about her until 1998, 40 years after Barkerville was rescued from its demise and became a heritage town. Most of these reports have come from guests who stay at the St. George Hotel.

Thomas Schoen and his wife, Bettina, secured the lease to the St. George (formerly known as the Nicol Hotel) in 1997 and renovated it in preparation for the following season. They heard about their ghostly visitor soon after they opened.

A guest woke Thomas and Bettina at 2:30 one morning, apologetic, but clearly upset. He told them that he and his wife were leaving immediately because his wife had seen a "presence." Not surprisingly, they didn't want to share their room with an extra guest.

During the next six years, Thomas got five or six reports of sightings every season, and they were far more specific than the first. The apparition usually appeared wearing a long white nightgown, sitting on one of the beds in Room 2. With the exception of that first startled guest, she always appeared to men.

A strange incident in another room made Thomas jokingly surmise the blonde got bored with sitting on the bed in Room 2. One morning, a gentleman staying in Room 4 told Thomas his running shoes were missing. Both he and his wife insisted the shoes were in their luggage when they checked in and that he had not worn them since arriving. After speaking to Thomas, the couple went into breakfast. They chose a table at random, then pulled out their chairs to sit down. The gentleman turned pale. There on the floor, exactly where his feet would be when he sat down, were his runners. To add to the mystery, there was a piece of red fabric tucked inside one of the shoes. Flabbergasted, the man asked Thomas if this type of fabric had been used anywhere in the hotel. It hadn't—not since the hotel had been renovated, anyway.

There have been other reports of apparitions in Barkerville. Richard Wright, a respected local historian, looked into one of the reports himself. People told him they had seen the ghost of a young woman, always standing behind a curtain, on the second floor of the building next door to the St. George. This building, now known as Madam Fanny Bendixon's Saloon and Boarding House, had once been connected to the St. George by a second-floor walkway. Richard went into the building to investigate. He didn't see the young woman, but he says he definitely felt some kind of energy there.

Neither Richard nor Thomas has ever seen apparitions, but the historian's investigation did not disprove the appearances, and Thomas believes his guests' reports. He doesn't try to keep the ghost stories secret, but he doesn't promote them either. Just as Alice Jowett had been, Thomas is a conscientious proprietor and wants his guests to be comfortable.

As far as we know, Alice, in her time, never had to contend with naughty spirits bothering her guests at the Windsor. It's certain she would not have approved of such antics then—or even now. If the Trout Lake ghost is indeed the Grand Old Lady of the Lardeau, guests don't have to worry about any brash trickery. The phantom is probably just checking to see that the guests are comfortable before she heads off over the lake to her precious Foggy Day mine.

Love in the Clouds

WHEN MARY AND LARRY LESLIE first met, they were both literally in the clouds. "The first time Larry mentioned getting married, I told him to come back tomorrow when he sobered up and ask me again," says Mary. "And he did."

Perched on their proverbial pink cloud, Larry and Mary dared not fall off. Their love nest was more than a mile high on a mountain that had made Hedley, BC, one of Canada's most prolific mining communities during the first half of the 20th century.

Larry and Mary lived in Nickel Plate Townsite, or "The Top," as it was dubbed, a community perched at more than 1,550 metres above sea level in a flat basin atop Nickel Plate Mountain. Nickel Plate, one of a range of mountains on the eastern side of the Similkameen Valley in British Columbia's southeastern interior, was a mountain of gold.

It was November 1941 when Larry, then 28 years old, was offered a steel sharpener's job at Nickel Plate mine. Three years earlier, he had left the famous Pioneer Mine in the Bridge River Valley and returned to the West Coast to work as a deckhand on a steamship. Although Larry was from the coast, he loved the mining life. So when a friend called him about a job with the "mine in the clouds," he jumped at the chance.

Mary, then 21, was the daughter of Nickel Plate miner Andrew Dzuris. Her family had been living on the mountain for eight years when Larry arrived. She worked in the cookhouse making sandwiches for the miners. Larry was one of many young bunkhouse miners who took an immediate shine to the pretty young miner's daughter. Mary jokes that Larry asked her out only because she made good peanut butter and sugar sandwiches, but—after 60 years of marriage—she has to admit there was more to it than that.

When they first started dating, Mary and Larry were not thinking much about what the future had in store for them or their community. They certainly could not have imagined they would be the last couple to leave the little town 14 years later. But the mountain wouldn't continue yielding its precious metal forever. Nickel Plate had been producing since gold-rush days—it already had a remarkable history.

Prospectors had been looking for gold in the Similkameen Valley since the 1860s when the yellow metal was found in Twenty Mile Creek. However, it wasn't until 1898, when independent prospectors Conrad Arundel and Frank Wollaston discovered gold on Nickel Plate Mountain, that the gold rush began. The pair quickly sold their interests on the mountain to Montana mining magnate M.K. Rogers for a reported $60,000. The following year, with big American money propelling the new mining venture, development began at the mine site. There were to be two mines on Nickel Plate Mountain: the Nickel Plate Mine, which began operating in 1904, and the Hedley Mascot Gold Mine, which started up in 1936.

The mines' greatest challenge was their location: 1,220 metres above Hedley, where a full-scale stamp mill and refinery were to be built. It was impossible to build a railway to deliver ore from the mine site to Hedley, so engineers convinced the company to construct a cable tramway—the longest mine tramway in the world.

But in the early 1900s, no manufacturer could guarantee a continuous steel cable of more than three kilometres. So the engineers decided to build two tramways: the first running 1,220 metres from the top to a halfway point called "Central Station" or the "knuckle," and the second running 1,700 metres from the halfway point to the tipple at the base of the mountain. The giant pulley system was an outstanding success. The cable pulled large, open cars, each with a five- or six-ton capacity, up and down the mountain with great efficiency. These cars ran on gravity. When the cars reached the bottom, they were unloaded. The system was then reversed, and the empty cars were sent back up.

Since there was no road that went directly between Hedley to the townsite at that time, miners and their families were allowed to ride in the cars on top of the ore. The passengers would spread old blankets or newspapers on the precious cargo to protect their clothes, then enjoy the spectacular ride as best they could. Safety regulations were strict and passengers required a pass, but it wasn't dangerous, as long as people didn't try to climb off.

Albert Etty, a former Nickel Plate resident who used to operate the tramline at Central Station, remembers a group of ladies—wives of wealthy shareholders—who wanted to ride in the ore cars so they could get an aerial photograph of Hedley and the Similkameen Valley. "They were big shots, but they really wanted a picture. I told them they couldn't climb off, so they sat on top of the ore car in their fancy white suits and got their shots," says Albert. "When we got down they bragged to everyone—even though their suits were no longer quite as spotless."

By 1904, the tramline had been completed and the mine was in production. Hedley became a bustling town with six hotels, churches, a bank, a school, a newspaper (the *Hedley Gazette*) and telephone, electrical and water services. It was named after Robert Rist Hedley, manager of the Hall

Smelter in Nelson. Mr. Hedley had lent his support—or "grubstaking"—to American surveyor Peter Scott, who was one of the first prospectors to stake Nickel Plate Mountain.

In 1909, the Canadian Northern Railway provided a branch line to Hedley. Now, the golden ore, which was coming out of the mines at a rate of more than 50,000 ounces a year, could be transported from Hedley by train.

Decent housing and amenities were scarce during Nickel Plate Townsite's early years, but with time it began to look and feel like a real community. Eventually there were company homes for families and bunkhouses for single men, a commissary and a community hall with a two-lane bowling alley, pool tables and a gym. For outdoor recreation, there was a small baseball field and courts for tennis and badminton. In winter, the courts were flooded to make a skating rink. There was also a small ski hill west of the school by an ore dump.

The natural beauty of the place was stunning. In any direction residents looked, they could see alpine forests, benches and valleys. They made the most of these surroundings by hiking and hunting. Although most residents loved living on the mountaintop, they found the isolation and the wildly unpredictable weather hard to deal with. "They used to have a saying that there were three months of winter and nine months of bad weather," says Larry. "You could get snow at any time of the year up there." And, as Mary can attest, they often did.

"When the snow melted in the spring, I thought I would

plant some vegetables. They came up beautifully, but then the next month, there was more snow," she says. "The last year we were there, it snowed every month of the year."

Despite the bad weather and isolation, people still came to live in Nickel Plate Townsite. At its peak, there were 50 houses and 200 full-time residents. These residents were more than pleased when the Nickel Plate–Hedley Road was built in 1937. There were more than 30 switchbacks, but residents favoured this direct route over the old road, which ran down the back side of the mountain. Although it was a heart-stopping journey, it cut the driving distance between the mountain perch and Hedley from 85 kilometres to 15. During the summers, the miners ran a bus service.

Larry and Mary drove into Hedley together often, but on their wedding day—six months after their first date—they travelled to the town separately. It was a happy day for both of them, except for the one anxious hour Larry spent waiting for Mary and wondering if she had changed her mind at the last minute.

"I was all dressed and waiting for the car to pick me up. I was a little nervous. I thought they had forgotten about me," says Mary. "They were well over an hour late, but they finally came. My friend had been celebrating too much the night before and almost forgot."

Their pink-cloud honeymoon period on top of Nickel Plate Mountain was brief. Larry got called for duty in the Second World War. After the war, the young couple lived in Vancouver for a few years but returned to Nickel Plate Townsite in 1949. Larry was promoted to the machine shop and the couple, who had started a family by then, stayed until 1955—the year the company decided underground mining was no longer feasible.

Together with the Mascot Mine, Nickel Plate Mountain yielded $50.3 million from the more than 1.7 million ounces of gold, 190,000 ounces of silver and more than 2,000 tons of copper between 1904 and 1955.

When the company decided to close the mine, Larry was asked to stay behind to oversee the selling of the assets. It was a sad and eerie few months for the young family. Their friends left one by one until they were alone. Then they watched the townsite being dismantled.

"When the children were playing outside, their voices echoed all over the hillsides," says Mary. When Larry had completed his final task on Nickel Plate Mountain, he moved his family to other mining locales, including Phoenix in the Boundary Country.

The Nickel Plate Mine had one more burst of production when it operated as a strip mine between 1987 and 1996. By then the mine was finally played out, and it closed for good. Mining is now a memory in Hedley, but the historic gold town has become a popular tourist centre. As of 2004, there is another tourist attraction in the area. The Mascot Gold Mine ruins have been restored, and the site is open to visitors. The old wooden buildings, clinging precariously to the almost vertical face of Nickle Plate Mountain, are a truly spectacular sight.

When Larry retired from mining, he and Mary decided to come back to the Similkameen Valley. Along with about 350 other residents, they have now made Hedley their permanent home. The couple have visited Nickel Plate Townsite since they returned, but there is very little to show that a community once flourished there. But they don't need buildings to remind them of what was so special about the place—they just need each other.

Dreamers

AS TOM GUTENBURG LOOKED AROUND the Gold Rush Rock Shop—a derelict store in a lonely old ghost town—he felt an immediate connection to the former owner. He had never met the man, Louie Skutnik, but he knew instinctively that the old prospector had been a dreamer. What he didn't know on that day in 1997 was that he would soon own the store and the entire ghost town of Bradian, just as Louis had.

"There was really nothing of value in there except a few chunks of jade," says Tom. "But there were receipts from when [Louis] panned gold, and when he sold the gold at the end of the year. The receipts show he didn't make much money, just a few thousand dollars a year, and this comprised his entire year's efforts at panning gold. He was as close to a pioneering spirit as you can get."

This visit to the ghost town of Bradian was the beginning of Tom's own dream. He and his wife became interested in British Columbia's mining history when they moved from Toronto to Vancouver 10 years earlier. There was no shortage of mining history in the scenic Bridge River Valley, where up to 10,000 miners had lived and worked over a period of 40 years, until the Bralorne mine closed in 1971.

"I kept going back to the old ministry of mine books because they were extremely descriptive. They had diary entries of people who would go and check out mining claims. It included their journeys and their stories, and I decided that I had to go and see all of these places."

These diary entries give just a hint of the prospectors' lives. British Columbia had attracted dreamers since 1858, when thousands of high-spirited adventurers began trudging northward. Louie was one such dreamer.

Louie (Ludwig) brought his family to Canada in 1965. The Austrian was fascinated with the idea of mining for gold, so headed to the gold-mining area of Bralorne, 225 kilometres north of Vancouver in the Bridge River Valley. He hoped to get a job as a miner, but could not pass the medical due to an old war wound. Undeterred, Louie staked the first of his placer claims. Using old-fashioned equipment, he started prospecting the pioneer way. To support his family until he "struck it rich," he worked for the mining company as a plumber and odd-job man.

Louie spent every spare moment panning for gold and jade. On weekends, he took the family to the rivers and streams with him. His daughter Irene, who now lives in Williams Lake, British Columbia, remembers those outings well.

"We wore hip waders, boots and rubber gloves that always seemed too short. It was incredibly cold as the water was glacier fed. My fingers would get numb. I remember the boots being up to my knees and still, you'd bend over too far and the water would slide down inside and soak your feet until they, too, became numb. When I think back on it now it sounds romantic, and in many ways it was very therapeutic. You couldn't talk for the noise of the river and the two motors running. You had a lot of time to think. When the motors stopped, be it from running out of gas or because of mechanical problems, you got to understand the meaning of silence being deafening. The roar in the ears was loud and would sometimes take days to completely go away."

Louie didn't make any big finds, but he was hooked. After a few years, he moved his family to Brexton, a deserted town six kilometres north of Bralorne. Here, he rented a house and opened his first rock shop. He made jewellery from gold nuggets and small chunks of jade and sold it to the seasonal residents and outdoorsmen who frequented the beautiful alpine wilderness.

In 1971 the Bralorne mine closed; the town and its five subdivisions became ghost towns almost overnight. The following year, Whiting Brothers of Vancouver bought all the sites, intending to turn the area into a year-round recreational resort. But the grand scheme fell through when it became apparent that few people were interested in travelling four hours from Vancouver, much of it over steep, winding roads.

Seeing an opportunity to own his own home and his own store, Louie purchased one of the sites—the entire 54-acre subdivision of Bradian. He constructed the Gold Rush Rock Shop from the houses that had fallen into disrepair and set up business. He remained there, contentedly making jewellery and prospecting, until he died in 1995.

Louie's family and friends remember him as a man with boundless energy and enthusiasm. His zeal for mining and dreams of striking it rich never diminished. Right to the end, he believed that the big find was waiting for him around the next bend of the creek.

Tom Illidge, a Bralorne miner and long-time friend of Louie's, remembers him fondly. "He was a great, happy-go-lucky guy who always had big dreams. He never got to be a millionaire, but he sure was happy trying." Tom knew many other dreamers in the area, including his friend Harry Street. This prospector realized his big dream in 1969 when he found a four-ton boulder of nephrite jade in a local creek. Valued at $50,000, it was the largest jade boulder ever found anywhere in the world. Tom will never forget the excitement of that find—he had helped Harry dig out the boulder with a loader.

Louie's story is a classic example of how a man followed his dream. Tom Gutenburg's story is an equally compelling example—and he is still dreaming.

Tom didn't learn about Louie's story during his first visit to Bradian, and he hadn't known about Bradian until he saw it in 1992. Tom and Kathleen were in the area to explore the historic Pioneer Mine near Bralorne. Because Bradian was not on the map, they didn't even know it existed. The ghost town intrigued them. It was set out along six streets, much like an average subdivision in any urban centre. Tom learned that at its peak, Bradian had been home to more than 200 people in 80 homes.

"It was very interesting because, being out in the middle of nowhere, the houses were right beside each other, maybe 25 feet separating each house and there was about 40 left," says Tom. The Gutenburgs were pleased to see the townsite so relatively well preserved. They had been to many former mining locales, including the Lardeau, Slocan and Kootenay regions of the province. They were saddened by the slow and sad demise of British Columbia's pioneer history, including the gradual ransacking of ghost towns for priceless historical artifacts. They had also witnessed the effects of apathy. Time and the elements had already claimed long-forgotten settlements. They hoped this would not be Bradian's fate.

The couple became fascinated with Bradian and Bralorne and learned more about the area's history. Large-scale gold mining began there in 1932 when Bralorne Mines Ltd. poured its first ingot. It weighed 393 ounces and was worth more than $6,000. In 1943, it was calculated that Bralorne had already paid almost one-sixth of the dividends earned by all the lode gold–mining operations in the previous 50 years. By 1948, the mine's value on the stock exchange was listed at $5 million. By 1971, when gold prices fell and mine officials scuttled operations, more than 4 million ounces of gold and 1.2 million ounces of silver had been produced— more than from any other mining operation in British Columbia. Within four decades, the Bralorne mines had yielded more than $32 million in dividends.

Tom also learned that as one group of dreamers left Bralorne, other groups arrived. Their plans varied between the grandiose and the bizarre. A proposed cooperative venture called the Gold Dust Twins Settlement Society wanted to turn the company's 1,400-acre holding into a community of craftsmen and environmentalists. However, the proposal fell through when the group couldn't secure government financing.

Another group of independent businessmen leased the main mine shaft and started a mushroom-growing operation. Although the mushrooms grew to near record-setting sizes in the dark, humid conditions, the logistical problems of getting them to markets doomed the venture.

Five years after his first visit to Bradian, a chance discussion rekindled Tom's fascination with the ghost town. By a stroke of luck—the kind of luck prospectors dream of—he heard it was for sale. He was flabbergasted that someone could actually own a whole town and immediately began speculating on whether he and Kathleen could buy it. With this thought in mind, they returned to Bradian. They were moved and shocked at what they saw. There were only 30 homes left, 10 fewer than five years earlier.

"When we got there we saw one guy tearing down one of the houses and another was chainsawing one apart. I thought it was a real shame. If I could have said, 'Stop this right now,' I would have—but I didn't own it," says Tom. "They didn't do anything but chainsaw it apart, and that is how they left it. They didn't even take anything. It would have been different if they had a purpose."

It was during this visit that Tom explored Louie's old store. If Louie had been able to give Tom advice, there is no doubt the old prospector would have urged him to follow his dream. Tom decided to try his luck. He began negotiations and crossed his fingers.

Six months later, Tom and Kathleen finalized the deal. They had purchased the ghost town for just under $100,000. Their first priority was to fix as many of the remaining houses as they could, and as quickly as possible. By the time they took possession, there were only 22 homes left.

The energetic couple set about repairing and painting

the houses. By the end of the second summer, they had fixed a third of the homes. Bradian's pioneer homes were now stabilized and, just as important, more secure from vandals and scavengers. They then converted one house for their summer home. The former miner's home is cozy and fitting for the Gutenburgs' lifestyle. Tom and Kathleen hope that other people who are interested in the province's mining heritage will visit Bradian. However, they might get more company than they expected.

In 2003, mining once again started in the Bralorne area, and Tom Illidge, Louie's friend, got a job there as a shift boss. It may come to pass that Bralorne's good old days will return, and along with them a new influx of prospectors looking to find that special golden nugget. Bradian might benefit, too. It is, after all, still a community of dreams.

A Halloween Prayer

TOTAL DARKNESS PRESSED IN ON Henry Wenzel as he sat, alone and helpless, 15,000 metres below the surface of the mine. His miner's lamp lay on the ground, flattened by one of the boulders that had crashed in on him during the cave-in. In the dead silence, he pondered his uneasy relationship with God.

He knew he would die slowly and painfully in this underground tomb unless help came quickly. His left arm felt cold and lifeless—it had been completely crushed. With his right hand, he gradually manoeuvred the mangled limb in front of him. Pain seared through his body and left him breathless. He stopped to gather his strength and collect his thoughts. He reached an inescapable conclusion. The arm was a useless impediment. If he were to have any chance of getting himself out of the tunnel, the arm would have to come off. He reached for the small knife he always carried in his back pocket and began to cut into his flesh.

The pain was unbearable. He couldn't do it. Half unconscious, his mind swam. Horrors he had experienced during the war crowded in on him. He thought of the Russian front, the bombings, the atrocities. For the umpteenth time, Henry wondered how any God could ever allow such pain and misery to go on in the world. He had considered praying in those dark hours of the war, and he thought about it now. But he dug in. He hadn't prayed then, and he wouldn't pray now.

Henry's daughter, Heidi, who was 10 years old at the time of her father's accident in 1960, became well aware of Henry's determination not to ask for God's help. "One day, years after the cave-in, we were all sitting around chatting and my dad started talking about when he was trapped in that tiny little coffin of a rocky cave. Putting the thumb and forefinger of his right hand close together, he said, 'I was this close to asking God for help.' After a pause he added, 'No. I wasn't going to do it!'"

Heidi will never forget the date of her father's ordeal because it was Halloween night—October 31, 1960. At 3:30 that afternoon, Henry had set off from his home in Britannia Beach to go to work at the Mount Sheer copper mine. As usual his wife, Elisabeth, had promised Henry there would be a nice warm meal waiting for him when he got home at midnight.

But Henry felt uneasy. For the past couple of days he'd had strange premonitions—a feeling of dread that something terrible was about to happen at the mine. "He mentioned it to my mom before he went," says Heidi. "He really didn't want to go, but he didn't want to lose a day's pay."

Henry had started working as a miner in 1954, soon after he arrived in Canada from his native Germany. His first job had been at a gold mine in Wells, BC. Two years later he moved to Britannia Beach to work at the copper mine. He was a "mucker," a man who went below specifically to clean up the ore and debris that had been mined by the previous shift. It was hard, backbreaking work, but it provided for his family.

Henry was known as a quiet, practical kind of man who believed in a stable family lifestyle and hard work. But his life had been anything but stable. He was born in 1916, during the First World War. His father had been killed in that war while Henry was still an infant. Henry grew up in the small village of Schlarpe, 100 kilometres south of Hanover. He became a baker, but when the Second World War broke out he was called up. Eventually, he was sent to fight on the eastern front. There he was captured by the Russians and sent to a Siberian prisoner-of-war camp.

The young soldier had already witnessed enough horrors during combat, but there was worse in store at the camp—

beatings, torture, disease and hunger. Inevitably, he became ill. "The Russians thought he had malaria," says Heidi. "They shipped him back to Germany so they wouldn't have to bury him. He weighed just over 90 pounds."

While Henry was thinking about his life—and possible death—in the mine, Heidi and her brother Manfred were thinking only of ghosts and goblins. Halloween was one of the highlights of the year for all the children in Britannia Beach. They were running from house to house, loading up their sacks with goodies. The sound of firecrackers and laughter filled their ears, so they didn't hear the low distant rumble from Mount Sheer—the dark, benevolent guardian that loomed over the townsite.

The explosion ripped through the mine at 6:45 p.m., sending 6,000 tons of rock into the underground area where Henry was working with his partner, Tom Archibald. The blast knocked Henry to the floor and burst his left eardrum. Rocks and debris showered down on him and shredded the ligaments in his left leg. Three-metre by three-metre timber roof supports snapped, and huge slabs of stone, one of them about 12 metres long and 7 metres wide, came crashing down. Fortunately, they jammed and came to a shuddering stop before reaching Henry, leaving him trapped in an alcove under one of the mammoth boulders. Tom barely managed to escape the cave-in. Knowing Henry's situation was desperate, he frantically sought help.

Heidi recalls that around 10 p.m., there was a knock at

their front door. "We were getting ready for bed, blissfully tired, when we heard the knock. My mother, visibly shaken, brought us into the kitchen and told us what had happened. We weren't given any information on my father's condition, only that his voice could be heard faintly through the rubble. I don't remember feeling great anguish or fear, but I do remember going into my bedroom and quietly asking God to please help my father."

Inside the mine, 30 miners were involved in the frantic race to save Henry Wenzel's life. As the rescue team tunnelled towards him, Henry yelled directions. Finally, after seven hours, the rescuers—and a doctor—reached Henry. He was lucky to be alive. Were it not for a twist of fate, he would have bled to death. The debris that had pulverized his left arm had also crushed his artery, cutting off the flow of blood.

Dr. Barrie Flather, a man who had never been inside a mine, crawled four metres through a tiny tunnel to give Henry medical attention. When he reached the stricken miner, he knew immediately the arm would have to be amputated. However, when the rescue mission began he had been told Henry probably wouldn't need any kind of surgery, so he hadn't brought his surgical equipment. All he had was a first-aid kit and a pair of scissors.

The doctor gave Henry morphine to dull the excruciating pain he was about to suffer. The narcotic fogged Henry's mind, but he was still conscious. The stalwart man cried out only once as the doctor finished the job Henry had started hours earlier. Dr. Flather amputated Henry's arm with scissors. Later, the doctor admiringly referred to Henry as a "very tough bird" because he had stood the pain so well. As soon as Henry had recovered sufficiently, the rescuers guided him out of the tunnel and back to safety. His ordeal was over. About an hour later, he was in a Vancouver hospital.

The dramatic rescue made the headlines, and Dr. Flather, George Preissler and John Johnson later received awards and citations for their heroics, including the coveted George Medal, which was awarded by Governor General Georges Vanier.

"In the days and weeks that followed the rescue, I made another request to God," says Heidi. "I asked would he please help my father grow his arm back. Indeed, in my childlike world, this was not an impossibility. Naturally this wish wasn't granted but it was a comforting one, nonetheless, and one I clung to until I was strong enough to let it go."

Henry was back at work eight months later. He didn't go back underground. Instead he worked in the mine mill, where the copper ore was concentrated. The "tough bird" learned to swim and drive a car with one arm. A few years later, while still working in the mill, he moved his family to a farm, where he cared for 22 hives of bees. The former miner enjoyed the peace and fresh air of the countryside and stayed on the farm until he died in 1980—20 years after the accident.

Henry's family was grateful to have him for that extra 20 years. Heidi is particularly grateful to the brave men who saved her father's life, as well as to the God of her understanding, who she believes answered her Halloween prayers. "If my father was still alive, I would really try to talk to him about God. I think life teaches us that eventually we have to surrender. Dad came close, but he didn't do it. He was kind of proud, thinking, 'Do you know what? I'm going to fight you.'" The old soldier did fight, and he won his toughest battle in his own way.

Henry Wenzel's rescue became part of the Britannia Beach history—almost 60 years' worth of history. Miners began to drift to Britannia Beach in the early 1900s when it was just a fledgling copper-mining camp. The rush for fame and fortune in the Howe Sound, 52 kilometres northwest of Vancouver, started in 1888 when an eccentric Scottish-born doctor named Alexander Forbes discovered copper on Britannia Mountain. He made the discovery entirely by chance. While hunting, he shot a deer. As he knelt by the wounded animal, Forbes noticed copper ore in the gravel. Or at least that was the doctor's story. Legend has it that he had been tipped off about the site by a local fisherman, but paid him $400 to keep quiet.

Forbes eventually sold his share in the discovery, but news of the find continued to fuel interest in the area. However, investors were slow to sink their money in the venture, and it was 1904 before the Britannia Mining and Smelting

Company shipped the first load of ore to Vancouver Island for production. The next year witnessed full production, and the mine's two communities, Britannia Beach and Jane Camp, were expanded. But the prosperity that continued into the First World War collided with a series of devastating calamities.

In 1915, management at Britannia was expecting a record year. Jane Camp, situated 1,524 metres above sea level on the east side of Britannia Mountain, was bearing the fruits of the company's success. The company began construction on a large scale. Men eagerly began work on a new bunkhouse, a locomotive repair shop, an enlarged powder house, a three-storey store and 20 employee cottages. In Britannia Beach, meanwhile, the company built 19 new cottages, a warehouse, a wharf and a telegraph office.

But at midnight on March 21, as miners were changing shifts, disaster struck. A massive mudslide more than 300 metres wide and almost two kilometres long roared into Jane Camp. The mud, rock, ice and snow pulverized everything in its path. It swept away the service buildings, miners' cottages and the railway terminal.

Two days later, the *Vancouver World* newspaper published an eyewitness report given to them by a miner, Harry Baxter. "It blew like the furies and in about two seconds there was a noise which the boys thought was 800 cases of explosives going off in the magazine. God knows how many poor miners have gone. The work of rescue was a hard thing.

We came to where Tom McCulla lived. He was jammed in between the timbers of his house with rocks piled all around. He called to us, and we got him out. He asked us to help him get his wife and daughter out. We found them, too. They were both dead."

When it was over, 57 men, women and children had been killed. Another 22 were missing. After Alberta's Frank Slide disaster of 1903, it was the most devastating landslide in Canadian history.

Company officials were quick to rebuild, and another townsite was constructed, albeit at a lower and safer elevation—720 metres above sea level. It was first known as Tunnel Camp, then as the Townsite and finally as Mount Sheer. Despite the landslide tragedy, Britannia's fortunes continued to soar throughout the First World War. By 1918, Britannia was considered one of the leading copper producers in the world.

By the end of the year, however, the Howe Sound mining communities were being ravaged by the worldwide Spanish influenza epidemic. Dozens of miners and their families were stricken. The mountain community hall was converted into a morgue, and the sick were transferred to the beach site. Many residents were then transported by ship to Vancouver hospitals. By the time the deadly virus finally subsided, 50 Britannia miners and residents were dead.

Three years later, while residents were still recovering from the influenza tragedy, Britannia Beach was struck by another calamity. Oil inside Mill No. 2 caught fire, causing catastrophic explosions. The mill was ultimately lost. Although the fire did not claim any lives in the community of 800 citizens, it caused more than $1.5 million damage to company property.

Seven months later, on October 28, a torrential rainstorm flooded the Lower Mainland. The rampaging waters cut Britannia Beach in half, smashing and carrying off buildings from their foundations. When it was over, another 37 Britannia Beach citizens were dead and 15 injured. In spite of the multiple tragedies of landslide, fire, influenza and flood, neither the company nor the people of Britannia would give up their hopes and dreams. The beach community was rebuilt.

A new mill was also constructed and was quickly surpassing daily production goals. In 1923, Britannia produced 22 million pounds of copper and 113,000 ounces of silver and gold. Six years later, Britannia had more than 1,100 men working underground, and the company broke more production records. In 1929, the Britannia mines were the largest copper producers in the British Commonwealth. Over the next decade, the company added zinc and pyrite to its production portfolio. The Second World War years witnessed an increased demand for strategic metals, and production increased once again with a still larger workforce.

Britannia's increasing good fortunes convinced many people to move to the beach community. Among them was a young couple with three children, Grace and Harry Adams. Harry was an assistant electrician foreman. His son Ernie was nine years old at the time and quickly learned to love the Beach. He still talks about the Beach's warm community spirit. "In 1945 you could leave your door wide open, and if a kid was in trouble he could go to people for help. If you hurt yourself you could go to anyone and they would put a Band-Aid on. They would give you a cookie, invite you in for coffee, or chat. It was a beautiful town to grow up in."

Ernie, who stayed in the area and worked at Britannia as a young man, is now aware that although Britannia Beach was an ideal community, it was far from perfect environmentally. Unfortunately, no one ever questioned what mining did to the environment in those days—it was simply accepted.

At the time of Henry Wenzel's rescue, Britannia's fortunes were slipping. The Mount Sheer townsite was dissolving in 1958, and the Britannia Mining Company went into receivership the following year. The Anaconda Mining Company took over in 1963, but mine operations were reduced. Eleven years later, with operating costs and taxes escalating and ore reserves dwindling, the last shift was called on November 1, 1974.

While 55 men went underground, the whistle blew a three-minute requiem for the Britannia Mines. A year later, the BC Museum of Mining was opened, and in 1988 Britannia was designated a National Historic Site.

Today, Britannia Beach is a quiet town of 400. This

population swells from time to time when former residents return to attend reunions. Heidi and her old friends love "going home." They look at the old buildings, walk some of the trails and rekindle memories of the joys and sorrows of their childhood.

Unlike so many other former mining towns, Britannia Beach is a proud tribute to British Columbia's mining heritage and to the families who gave their hearts—and sometimes their lives—to mining.

The Deer Hunter

HARVEY GODFREY LOVED THE FOLKLORE of Vancouver Island's east coast—even though it made him feel "creepy." He learned some of that lore as a child when his mother told him stories about the Wild Man who dug for clams at the end of the beach.

Harvey's son, Russ, also heard his grandmother talk about the strange creature who looked for food along the shore of Qualicum Beach and down to where Parksville is today. Locals say he was first seen coming out of the wilderness around 1900.

Russ, who still lives on Vancouver Island, assumes his grandmother was talking about the Sasquatch. He asked her about it when he was a teenager, but she told him she hadn't seen Sasquatch—or the Wild Man. She had just been told as a child not to go up to the end of the beach because the Wild Man had often been seen there. She didn't seem to find anything strange in that at all.

Harvey believed that the legendary creature, also known as Big Foot, really did exist. He never dismissed any of the seemingly wild legends: stories of the supernatural, tales of lost treasures or the multitude of island stories about ancient Spanish gold hunts. Perhaps this is why he always made a point of being aware of who and what was around him, especially during his countless trips into the bush. He was an expert hunter, and his favourite stomping grounds were the forests in and around Leechtown, a scenic hour's drive from downtown Victoria, and one of Vancouver Island's most celebrated pioneer gold-rush ghost towns.

When Harvey was a young teen in the 1930s, his primary job was hunting for game. While his dad ran the farm and his mother looked after the garden, Harvey headed to the mountains and hills with his rifle or bow.

"My dad was a killer shot," says Russ. "Even my cousins who went out with him couldn't believe the shots my old man could make. There would be a deer on the other side of the river on a slash that you could barely see, and he would look through his scope, and bang, he got him."

When Harvey was a young man, Leechtown was a logging community. He knew deer were plentiful in the area so he often hunted there. As well as bagging his fair share of game, he developed a keen interest in the area's folklore. He especially enjoyed the tales of the 19th-century gold rush and lost treasures that revolved around the town's namesake, Lt. Peter Leech of the Royal Engineers—the first man to find gold on the bars of the Sooke River in July 1864.

The British officer wrote about the area eloquently: "The diggings extend for a full 25 miles, and would give employment to more than 4000 people. The country abounds with game and the honest miner need never fear but that he could find food without much trouble. The whole value of the diggings cannot be easily overestimated. The gold will speak for itself."

The discovery ignited an unparalleled rush for gold on the island and West Coast. It included the frenzied arrival of veteran prospectors barely recovering from the celebrated rushes in California and the Cariboo.

By November, 1,200 miners were at work. A townsite was created on the flats, first named Kennedy Flats, where the newly named Leech River and Sooke River converged. It could accommodate up to 5,000 people. Despite the early pandemonium, the motley mix of gold-crazed prospectors and government officials was later described by Gold Commissioner Richard Golledge as "exceedingly well-behaved."

However, the adventurers still liked to celebrate. Soon, the town boasted 30 saloons and dance halls. Merchants sold liquor in tents, and hotels hosted all-night roulette and poker parties. Unfortunately, Leechtown's boom was short-lived. Although an estimated $100,000 was taken out during the first frantic year, miners began heading for richer prospects by 1865.

For the next 140 years, Leechtown continued to stir the imaginations of people who had a passion for gold or an interest in folklore. The stories go back to before Leechtown was established. One of these ancient tales is the widely debunked legend of "Rattlesnake" Dick Barter's $40,000 gold cache from a California mule-train robbery in 1856. Legend has it that the outlaw buried the treasure in Leechtown. One version of the tale says he put it in a knee-high rubber boot, covered with an inverted frying pan, near Leechtown's largest building. But historians have repeatedly pointed out there is no evidence to prove that the gold ever left the United States, or that "Rattlesnake" was ever on Vancouver Island.

Still, the strange Leechtown stories continued into the 1900s, amusing the few prospectors who still hoped to find gold. But the river had already relinquished most of its treasure. According to a provincial government report, only 192 ounces, worth $5,807, was discovered in the Leech River from 1921 to 1945.

From about 1900 to the 1950s, Leechtown was a logging community, at one time reaching a peak population of 250 residents. Tom Carlson, a former Vancouver Island resident who lived in Leechtown in the fifties, recalls how plentiful the game was in those days. "I remember men would take

Leechtown residents were shocked in 1951 when a spar tree fell and crushed the town store and post office. Tom Carlson is the child being carried in his mother's arms at the far right of the crowd.

turns going hunting, no matter what time of year it was. If you got a deer, you brought it back and hung it up in the lean-to. They would butcher it up and everyone shared it. You didn't have to worry about a hunting licence or deer tags or anything. We always had venison, always canned."

Leechtown was a far different place during its second go-round as a community. The excitement, romance and glamour brought by gold were long gone by 1950. Instead of the wild days of saloons and free-flowing liquor, it was more common to find workers sitting in living rooms quietly smoking. Not cigarettes, but opium. Tom says it wasn't at all unusual for the loggers to smoke opium. Nobody thought anything of it.

What the logging community did pause to think about was a near disaster in 1951, when a huge, overloaded spar tree, measuring about a metre and a half at its base, toppled and fell on the camp office-cum-store.

Tom, still a young child at that time, was sitting on his mother's knee inside their shack by the tracks, about 65 metres from the building. The force of the tree slamming down on the store rocked their home. "I remember the exact moment," says Tom. "You could hear the earth rumble when it hit. It was like an earthquake. There were only about 10 or 12 people hanging around. Nobody was inside at the time, and nobody was hurt."

A few years later, after a fire destroyed the mill, Tom and his family left Leechtown. By the end of the decade, it was all over for the former gold-rush town's second coming. Twice in a span of less than 100 years, Leechtown had become a ghost town.

But the hunters remained, and Harvey was one of them. During the 1960s, the avid outdoorsman took his son along on his hunting trips every chance he could. There wasn't much to see in Leechtown by then—just the odd foundation, a few shacks and old bottles and debris.

Russ was never keen on hunting, but he admired his

father's knowledge of the wilderness. Father and son hiked the gullies and ravines for hours, but never got lost. Along the way Harvey told tales of gold, lost treasures and strange sightings. He also regaled his son with tales of hunters being chased by white lights around Jordan Meadows, a triangular parcel of trees northwest of the former townsite. Russ says Harvey's stories were always believable because his father rarely embellished them.

During one of these trips to Leechtown, Harvey told Russ about his own eerie experience in nearby Jordan Meadows. It had happened a quarter century earlier, in the late 1930s. Apparently, Harvey had been walking in the bush for many hours and decided to stop for a cigarette and some lunch. While he was overlooking a slash, a peculiar feeling overcame him.

"He said the hair on the back of his neck stood up," says Russ. "He felt as if he was being watched." Out of no-where, Harvey heard a loud bell. At first the hunter thought it might be a train or a church, but the sound was too deep, like a gong. Whatever it was, Harvey also knew he was in the middle of the wilderness where there were no buildings or people. Five minutes later, Harvey turned and looked across the ravine. And there, on a small hill, stood a white horse. The fine animal was looking directly at him. He wondered whether the horse was lost.

He reflected on the animal's beauty, and remembered the white horse he'd had when he was a child. As he watched the horse, it turned and walked slowly back into the forest. Out of curiosity, Harvey crossed the ravine to where it had been standing. When he got there, there was no sign of the animal, nor any trace of tracks.

"It gave him the willies. He was a tracker," says Russ. "If a horse is in the woods, it is going to leave a trail, but there was nothing. A deer is a quarter of the size of a horse and you can hear it," he adds. "Deer are noisy in the woods and a horse walking through the woods is going to cause a lot more noise, but there was nothing but silence—and no tracks."

Harvey hiked around the area for a few hours looking for the horse, but it was nowhere to be seen. He linked up with his hunting partner and told him about the strange sighting. His friend suggested it could have been a "ghost horse." Harvey had never encountered anything like it in all his years in the woods, and he never saw it again. The incident would always baffle him. Years later, he heard about the bizarre story of a horse skeleton draped over a cairn of stones lying near the Sooke River. The phantom horse mystery became even more intriguing.

In 1959, Ted Harris, a reporter for the *Victoria Daily Colonist* newspaper, heard about a mysterious tunnel allegedly found by a prospector named Ed Mullard, also a deer hunter. After unsuccessfully tracking a deer, Mullard said he had stumbled upon a descending staircase in the brush. It led to a series of steps, seven in all, and beyond to an arch and rectangular gallery about three metres in height. Using only the tiny, flickering glow of matches, Mullard gingerly went down a second staircase and into the gallery. He spotted another arch, seven more steps and another gallery, but the tunnel was filled with water and his light was quickly fading. He left and never returned. Harris later made a pact with Mullard to see the tunnel in June of that year.

Unfortunately, Mullard died a month before their scheduled expedition. He had told no one, including Harris, the location of the tunnel. The newspaper sponsored an investigation to verify Mullard's discovery, but nothing came of it.

Folklore enthusiasts theorize that the tunnel may have been constructed by Spanish explorers as far back as the 16th century. Mullard's mythical tunnel added to the rumours of a lost Spanish cannon in Jordan Meadows, a bronze tablet embedded in the fork of a tree, and the legend of Bear Hill, located on the Saanich Peninsula, 12 kilometres north of Victoria. "Local Native legend says they had a pet bear that warned them of Spanish explorers sneaking up on encampments," says Russ. "The bear would let out a warning. Supposedly, the Spanish killed it with a musket."

Adding to the mysterious Spanish connections was an unusual relic unearthed by a friend's father when Russ was a child. At first, the man thought it was a rusted poker of some type, but the threading on one end suggested it was more like the hilt on a rapier or sword. "They kept it for years as a fireplace poker. I don't think they ever knew what it was," Russ adds. "It does give credence to the local legend about the Spanish being around here and doing a lot of exploring."

Harvey died in 1984 at the age of 64. A pilot friend flew over the Leechtown area and scattered Harvey's ashes over his hunting grounds on Mount Lazar. Harvey passed away still relishing the island's folklore and believing there was more to Leechtown than gold. Along with the phantom horse, Harvey has become part of that folklore.

CASSIAR

The Bond

LABOUR DAY WEEKEND, 1954: Joe Van Raalte was first off the boat and onto shore. He raced to Father Henk Huijbers, who was leaning against a fallen tree, drenched and gasping for air. Joe, already shaking and afraid, was terrified of hearing what the priest was about to say.

Between sobs and shivers, Father Huijbers cried out in anguish, "I lost him. I couldn't get him." Blood trickled from a cut on the side of his head and ran, unheeded, over his frozen features. The priest was in shock. He couldn't believe what had happened. "I had him. I had him," he kept repeating. "And I lost him."

Twelve-year-old Joe quietly turned away. He already knew it was true, but he didn't want to hear the dreadful words. For a few moments he stood by the riverbank and looked deep into the rushing current of the Liard River. His head swam and his thoughts drifted back over the last few golden days.

It was already parka weather in Cassiar on September 1. Joe and his 10-year-old brother, Bobby, knew what was coming. Their first winter in Cassiar had been a cruel shock compared to Toronto. The thermometer once dipped to -65°C, cold enough to freeze lungs solid within 30 seconds. The rule in Cassiar, located in the extreme northwest section of British Columbia, was that folks were to stay indoors unless it "warmed up" to -50°C. Cassiar's only saving grace was the absence of wind. The isolated northern British Columbia mining community was tucked in a bowl-like valley surrounded by 1,700-metre high mountains.

For most people in Cassiar, the extreme cold was a learning experience. Cassiar was a new town that had been established in 1952 on the hopes and dreams of a new asbestos-mining operation. Joe's father, Alfred "Van" Van Raalte, a draftsman, had been lured from Toronto in 1953 to be the town's structural construction superintendent. He uprooted his wife, Jean, and children, Joe, Bobby, Peggy, Beverly and Bruce—and brought them to the remote wilderness town. The devoted family man felt it would be a safer place to raise his kids.

In 1954, accommodations in Cassiar were basic. Single men were housed in two-man tents. Families lived in a residential section of the town, still referred to as the campsite. It was an old army barracks that had been used by road workers during the construction of the Alaska Highway. The buildings had been converted into multi-family units. This was where the Van Raaltes lived for the first two years.

As hard as Cassiar winters were, the summers were gorgeous, although too short and—for many—too infested with nasty blackflies. Joe and Bobby loved the northern summers and spent many days hiking and playing in the bush. Sometimes they found a special spot and sat in a patch of bitter but tasty mossberries. Armed with a box of sugar cubes, they shoved the cubes in their cheeks and gobbled the berries.

Those days were lazy, fun and forever memorable. Now that September had arrived, there was no time to waste. They were determined to make the most of the remaining good weather. So when the local priest, Father Huijbers, organized a four-day scout's camping trip up the Liard River for Labour Day weekend, they both wanted to go. Joe knew instinctively there might not be another chance to be a kid.

"There were only a handful of preteen boys in Cassiar. We were leaving childhood behind and this was sort of a rite of passage," says Joe, who now lives in Victoria. "It was a nice thing Father Huijbers had arranged. I think my brother and I were the only Catholics. He didn't differentiate."

Although both boys were chomping at the bit to go, there was a problem with Bobby. He was two years younger than the rest of the boys, and his parents and Father Huijbers felt he was too young to go. But Joe and Bobby were not only brothers, they were best friends, and Joe pleaded with his parents to let Bobby go on the wilderness adventure.

Jean looks back at that day and clearly remembers Bobby's determination. "He was so sure he was going, he said, 'I'm a big boy, I can look after myself.' There would have been no living with him if I'd kept him home from that trip." Jean and Van were reluctant to let Bobby go, but they consulted the priest—he was a man who had earned their respect and trust.

Father Huijbers had already made a strong impression and contribution to the fledgling community, and in particular to the Van Raalte household. He planned to build a church, but until the community had grown, mass was held in the Van Raalte living room. The 38-year-old Dutch-born priest was a sociable man who enjoyed chatting to other Cassiar residents and sharing his war stories. He had been a hero in the Netherlands during the Second World War, so had some interesting tales to tell.

While aiding the Dutch Resistance, he successfully evacuated two injured Allied pilots shot down over the Netherlands. He also assisted the wounded, members of the underground and others hunted by the Nazis. In 1943, he was arrested by the Gestapo, but escaped from the concentration camp the same night. Joe recounts the story: "While he was being chased one night, he ducked into a small cave and fell asleep. When he woke up he noticed a spider spinning a web across the mouth of the cave. The spider finished his web and Father Huijbers fell back asleep. A German patrol was looking for him. An officer told one soldier to check the cave. Father Huijbers figured he was finished. The guy came into the cave and got spider webs in his face. He told the officer he couldn't be in there as the cave was full of spider webs. He walked away."

When Father Huijbers came to Canada in 1947, he settled in the Yukon and helped build recreation halls, community clubs and churches. When Cassiar's ambitions were announced, the new town became the priest's mission. The priest was strong, and some found him intimidating, but adults felt he was a good role model for the boys. He was a big man—well over six feet tall—with a solid build and a heavy beard.

In 1954, Cassiar was still emerging as a community. Young boys and teens were scarce, and anyone who was Catholic was quickly enlisted by Father Huijbers to serve as an altar boy. With Father Huijbers using the Van Raalte living room for his temporary church, it was a convenient arrangement—although it had its tense moments.

"Fresh fruit and vegetables were really tough to get because it had to come by truck from Dawson Creek," says Joe. "Mom managed to get some fresh tomatoes that were supposed to be for our supper. Father Huijbers came by and asked for something to eat. He saw the tomatoes on the counter and ate them all. Mom was furious, but she was a good Catholic lady, and they don't deny priests anything."

Father Huijbers was also hesitant about letting Bobby go on the trip, but when the boys' parents reluctantly allowed it, he agreed to take the lad. After the decision had been made, Jean quietly continued to fret. Both her sons were filled with an abundance of nervous energy. Joe shook while Bobby fiddled. He would touch things unconsciously. He was a bona fide fiddler. He was also a fearless free spirit. This lack of fear had already led him close to disaster.

"Before we left Toronto, Bobby ran out of the house one day and across the road between two parked cars. I just stood still and held my breath because I could see a car coming," says Jean. "I told a neighbour I thought I would never raise that child. She said, 'I'm glad you know it.' You say these things but you don't really believe them."

Earlier that summer, Bobby had climbed on a mine conveyor belt to play. The belt began to carry him to the top of the 20-metre tower. Unknown to Bobby, the end of the ride meant falling into the bottom of an ore storage bin. This fall could have seriously injured or killed him. Luckily, before the boy was pulled to the top an alert miner spotted him and quickly shut down the conveyer belt.

Jean hoped her son could control his free spirit, at least during the four days of the fishing trip. When September 1 dawned, she had already waved goodbye to Joe and Bobby. They, along with three other scouts (Walter, Matti and Doug) were piled into two vehicles, heading out on the three-hour, 165-kilometre drive to Lower Post. Earl Wright,

Bobby Van Raalte (centre, holding a plate) and other Cassiar scouts and adults on the 1954 Liard River camping and boating trip. Father Henk Huijbers stands directly behind Bobby, while brother Joe stands beside them at right.

a mine shopkeeper, drove one of the vehicles, and Father Huijbers drove the other.

As soon as they got to Lower Post, the boys went to a general store and loaded up with junk food and fishing gear. The adults went to pick up Frank, a local man who provided ferry service in the area. The group quickly stowed their gear on the riverboat and headed upstream on the meandering Liard River. The boys were in a festive mood. Soon they would be dipping their fishing rods into the river, hoping to catch trophy-sized Dolly Varden and Arctic grayling, and having

128

fabulous pan-fried lunches onshore. Joe could not help but notice that Father Huijbers was the biggest adult onboard. Although Frank was steering the boat, the imposing priest was clearly the captain. Everybody looked up to him.

As the boat navigated the river, the boys marvelled at the sight of moose standing nonchalantly near the shore. Above them, they watched the non-stop flights of wilderness birds, no doubt heading south for winter. For Bobby and Joe, life was as perfect as it could be. At about 5:00 p.m., Frank turned the boat to shore. It was time to set up camp.

Father Huijbers told the boys to find firewood while he and the men unloaded the gear and supplies. He told the scouts to set up the tents and stay close to camp. As the boys dragged driftwood from the banks to camp, the adults brought out axes to chop logs. "They didn't trust us with axes, although we had chopped wood at one time or another," says Joe. "The adults were there to make sure nobody got hurt."

The boys were having the time of their lives. After chores, they fished for an hour before supper, then grouped around a roaring campfire. As kids love to do, they sang songs and told ghost stories.

Gradually the fire died down and Father Huijbers announced it was time for bed. Joe scrambled into his sleeping bag fully clothed. Bobby was beside him, quieter now that he was tired. For many minutes, Joe stared through the darkness at the tent roof. The low murmur of adult voices was the only sound he could hear. When the men stopped talking, the deafening silence of the wilderness closed in around him. For Joe, it was the perfect end to a perfect day.

Three more perfect, sunny days followed. When the fourth and final day arrived, the boys once again marvelled at yet another cloudless sky. Shortly before 9 a.m. they had packed up and were back on the Liard River. The boat moved swiftly in the fast-flowing water. It wouldn't take long to get back to Lower Post.

It was chilly on the river, so all the boys took turns sheltering in the wheelhouse, a covered cabin at the front of the boat, where Frank was steering. Joe sat sternside, behind the wheelhouse, while Bobby had his turn inside. Bobby, as usual, couldn't keep still. He moved to the port side of the cabin and leaned against the door, fiddling with the doorknob. His hands were cold, so he jammed them into his blue jean pockets. He then edged over to the port side and leaned against the door. It swung open.

The lad pulled his hands out of his pockets to grab on to something, but he touched nothing but air. His momentum carried him over the side of the boat. With his arms flailing, he was thrown into the frigid water.

Joe witnessed it all. He froze. He had seen his brother's eyes, wide with astonishment, as he fell through the air. Then he saw him go under. The boat was moving at 18 knots; Bobby was out of sight within seconds. When he reappeared, he was waving his arms and yelling for help. "By then he was 100 to 150 feet behind us. The boat was running with the current. He was too, but we were moving faster."

The adults jumped into action. Father Huijbers rushed to the stern of the boat. Fully dressed, he dived into the river and began swimming against the current towards Bobby. By then, the terrified boy was about 100 metres away. Earl gathered all the life jackets and handed them out to the boys. Frank wheeled the boat around and headed back towards Bobby. As the boat passed Bobby, the scouts threw all the life jackets overboard. Frank then handed the wheel to Doug, the oldest scout. Without hesitation, he dived into the water to help with the rescue. The boys were heartened to know that two adults were now swimming towards their friend. But Frank never surfaced. In his haste, he had dived straight into the boat's propeller. They never saw him again.

Doug frantically swung the boat around for another pass. Joe kept his eyes riveted on his little brother. Bobby had not managed to get to any of the life jackets and was appearing and disappearing under the waves. Father Huijbers closed in on him. As the boat completed its turn, the priest finally managed to grab the boy. But the boat was too close to them. The tail end clipped Father Huijbers' head, momentarily stunning him. He lost his grip on Bobby. The frigid water revived the priest in an instant. But in that brief interval, Bobby had disappeared. Frantic, the priest scanned the water in every direction—but he couldn't see the boy.

Doug turned the boat for another pass. Joe sat immobilized by shock on the starboard side of the stern. As the boat passed the spot where Bobby had last been seen, a limp hand reached over the gunwale at the other side of the boat, three metres from Joe. Before Joe could get there, his brother's hand had slid back under the gunwale. The horrifying scene is etched forever in Joe's mind.

Another search in the area proved fruitless, so the desolate group headed for the nearest shore. Father Huijbers stumbled ashore and wept. He had not been able to save Bobby, and Frank had drowned trying to help. He knew, without a doubt, they were both dead. However, for two hours, the men and boys searched the riverbank, hoping against hope that Bobby and Frank would somehow wash in alive. Finally, they gave up and boarded the boat. When they reached Lower Post, they got into their vehicles and drove to Watson Lake, where they reported the two drownings to the RCMP. It was a quiet journey. "I remember feeling nothing, absolutely nothing. I was still in shock," says Joe.

It was a month before Frank's body was recovered. Two weeks after that, Bobby's small body was found. Father Huijbers held a requiem high mass for him. So many people wanted to pay their last respects that the mass had to be held in the town's recreation centre. Joe was one of the altar boys.

"I couldn't go on at certain points. I had to stop. Father Huijbers was very understanding. Usually when I missed something, he would look at me with a frown on his face.

But at Bobby's mass, he waited for me to get over my immediate grief before he continued." At home, Joe grieved quietly with his family. For many months, they all dreamed of Bobby.

"We kept dreaming that he would come home," says Jean. "We all had the same dream, that he wasn't dead. He just went away."

Joe's dreams were nightmares. For the next 43 years he stumbled through life, the horrifying tape of his little brother's hand slowly slipping off the gunwale playing endlessly in his head.

The tragedy continues to haunt the Van Raalte family. Half a century later, Jean still dreams about Bobby. "You could see him coming towards you and then he's around and then he disappears again," she says. "Bobby is always gone by the end of the dream. I have talked to all the children about it, and they have had the same dreams."

Joe tried to bury the horror of 1954. He talked about it only to one trusted teacher, the doctors who tried to help him deal with it and his family. But the memories were not far below the surface. In 1997, during a casual coffee-room chat with a young co-worker at his Victoria office, the young woman asked him about Cassiar. Joe regaled her with stories about the northern frontier spirit and, of course, the mind-boggling cold. They chatted about mossberries and fishing. And then he told her about Bobby.

"While I was telling her, I broke up. She put her arms

around me like I was her child. I bawled like a baby," says Joe. "It was such a cleansing process. I just felt released."

Joe's healing continues, and he has begun to forgive himself. While 1954 can still bring tears, the nightmares have eased. Joe knows Bobby is listening somewhere, and his spirit guides his big brother's healing.

Guardians of the Ghosts

IT HAS BEEN A LONG, hard road for Joe, as well as for most other former residents of Cassiar. When the end came for the Cassiar mine and the townsite in 1992, residents felt angry and betrayed. When their homes and most other buildings in the community were bulldozed, they were outraged.

During the course of Cassiar's 40-year history, the northern community reached a maximum population of 2,500 citizens and over the years employed more than 30,000 workers. Despite the remote location, health worries over the long-term effects of asbestos and the notoriously cold winters, Cassiarites loved their community. More than a decade after its demise, they continue to hold the memories of their beloved town close to their hearts. Thanks to the dedication of two former Cassiarites, they can now "go home" on-line.

In 1998, former resident Simone Rowlinson built a website to honour her Cassiar heritage. Before her family moved to Cassiar, she had already felt the sting of losing a community when Pine Point, Northwest Territories, closed and was levelled. She knew former residents would appreciate having something that would remind them of the community and make it easy to stay in touch with old friends and neighbours.

Two years later, she handed the website over to Herb Daum, the first boy born in the northern interior mining town. In just a few years, the site has grown from five pages to hundreds. The former mining town has become Canada's first revived on-line ghost town—a "virtual" community.

For Herb, who lived in Cassiar from 1954 to 1983, the website is a labour of love. And it really is labour—he has devoted thousands of hours to it. He has posted hundreds of Cassiar-related photographs, sent newsletters, announced new members, updated the 900-member address book, posted news stories, promoted reunions and e-mailed obituary notices.

Herb says he gives his time willingly because Cassiar was his home and he wants to keep it alive. Even though maintaining the site has been frustrating and expensive, he finds it very rewarding.

"Fortunately, many Cassiarites truly appreciate the huge

effort I make on their behalf, and some have sent financial contributions to help cover the operating expenses and my time," says Herb. "I am very grateful to these Cassiar angels. Without their support, the website and newsletters would eventually cease to exist."

While Herb Daum devotes his efforts to Cassiar, John Kinnear continues to give his time to a ghost community far to the south. John is still trying to convince civic officials in the Fernie area to erect a commemorative marker to honour the 130 miners killed in the 1902 Coal Creek mine disaster. There is not a single plaque or marker at or near the Coal Creek townsite to honour the fallen miners in what was one of Canada's worst mining disasters.

As the wilderness reclaims the Coal Creek site, John feels there should be at least one monument to the men, women and children who lost their lives and their loved ones to the dangerous industry of mining. John feels, as do I, that although we cannot prevent nature from obliterating all tangible signs of the area's pioneer days, we can—and should—combat apathy that erodes the intangible pioneer spirit.

Bibliography

Basque, Garnet. *Ghost Towns and Mining Camps of the Boundary Country.* Surrey: Sunfire Publications Ltd., 1992.

Cox, Doug. *Mines of the Eagle Country—Nickel Plate and Mascot.* Penticton: Skookum Publications, 1997.

Glanville, Alice, ed. *Boundary History—The Thirteenth Report of the Boundary Historical Society.* Grand Forks: Boundary Historical Society, 1995.

LeBlanc, Suzanne. *Cassiar—A Jewel in the Wilderness.* Prince George: Caitlin Press Inc., 2003.

Norton, Wayne, and Naomi Miller. *The Forgotten Side of the Border—British Columbia's Elk Valley and Crowsnest Pass.* Kamloops: Plateau Press, 1998.

Parent, Milton, ed. *Circle of Silver.* Nakusp: Arrow Lakes Historical Society, 2001.

Paterson, T.W. *Ghost Town Trails of Vancouver Island.* Langley: Stagecoach Publishing Co. Ltd., 1975.

Paterson, T.W. *Ghost Towns and Mining Camps,* Langley: Sunfire Publications Ltd., 1989.

Paterson, T.W. *Lower Mainland—British Columbia Ghost Town Series.* Langley: Sunfire Publications Ltd., 1984.

Pellowski, Veronika. *Silver, Lead and Hell—The Story of Sandon.* New Denver: Prospectors' Pick Publishing, 1992.

Ramsey, Bruce. *Ghost Towns of British Columbia.* Vancouver: Mitchell Press Ltd., 1963.

Wright, Richard Thomas. *Barkerville—A Gold Rush Experience.* Williams Lake: Winter Quarters Press, 1998.

Index

Index

Acknowledgements

The author is indebted to the many officials from historical societies and organizations throughout British Columbia for their generous support to this project, particularly Rose Gobeil of the Boundary Historical Society; Rosemarie Parent of the Arrow Lakes Historical Society; Farrah Rooney, Curator of Education and Collections, BC Museum of Mining; Mike Ballantyne of the British Columbia Folklore Society; John Kinnear of the Fernie and District Historical Society; and Brent McBride, Access Services, BC Archives.

I want to also acknowledge the wonderful contributions of Lorraine Barr, a valued resource for the Waldo chapter. As well, I am grateful to Dr. Robert Lampard, historian and director of medical health of Red Deer's Michener Services, for generously allowing me to probe through his extensive private library. Special thanks go to Herb Daum, web master for the "Cassiar . . . do you remember?" website, for his support and never-ending enthusiasm. I want to especially thank my editor for this book, Pat Kozak, whose dedication and enthusiasm for this project has made me a better writer. I also want to express special gratitude to writers and historians Doug Cox of Penticton, BC; Richard Thomas Wright of Williams Lake, BC; Milton Parent of Nakusp, BC; as well as Lawrence Chrismas of Calgary. Writers can be prickly about helping other writers, but these four gentlemen were absolutely generous with their time and patience.

Most of all, I thank my wife, Darlis, and daughter, Darlana. Without their love, support and patience, this book would not have been possible.

About the Author

Johnnie Bachusky is a national award–winning journalist who has explored hundreds of ghost towns across western and northern Canada since the late 1990s. He has written dozens of ghost-town and heritage-related articles for newspapers and magazines in Canada. Johnnie is also the author of *Ghost Town Stories: From Renegade to Ruin along the Red Coat Trail* and *Ghost Town Stories of BC: Tales of Hope, Heroism and Tragedy*. His heritage photography has been featured in national and international publications, and he has been consulted and featured in many television and film documentaries. As well, he is the co-creator of three acclaimed websites about ghost towns in Alberta, Saskatchewan and British Columbia, as well as the heritage photography site Silent Structures. His photography of pioneer wooden grain elevators is also featured on many websites, including Grain Elevators of Canada. He lives with his wife, Darlis, daughter, Darlana, and his three cats and hound in Red Deer, Alberta.

More Great Books in the Amazing Stories Series

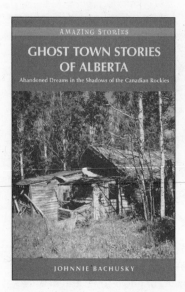

Ghost Town Stories of Alberta
Abandoned Dreams in the Shadows of the Canadian Rockies

Johnnie Bachusky

(ISBN 978-1-894974-72-1)

Today, many of the historic coal-mining ommunities of the Rocky Mountains are uninhabited ghost towns. Yet behind the crumbled ruins are tales of perseverance, danger and romance. A devastating mine explosion on Halloween shatters the lives of mining families in Nordegg. The miners of Mountain Park build a hockey rink still celebrated in local lore. A young immigrant couple in Mercoal establishes a successful business only to have their love story sadly cut short. These 11 dramatic and poignant ghost-town tales are sure to fascinate all who love pioneer history.

Also by Johnnie Bachusky:

Ghost Town Stories: From Renegade to Ruin Along the Red Coat Trail
(ISBN 978-1-551539-92-8)

Visit www.heritagehouse.ca to see the entire list of books in this series.